Architecture in Detail

Architecture in Detail

Graham Bizley

AMSTERDAM • BOSTON • HEIDELBERG • LONDON • NEW YORK • OXFORD
PARIS • SAN DIEGO • SAN FRANCISCO • SINGAPORE • SYDNEY • TOKYO
Architectural Press is an imprint of Elsevier

Architectural Press is an imprint of Elsevier
Linacre House, Jordan Hill, Oxford OX2 8DP, UK
30 Corporate Drive, Suite 400, Burlington, MA 01803, USA

First edition 2008

British Library Cataloguing in Publication Data
A catalogue record for this book is available from the British Library

Library of Congress Cataloging-in-Publication Data
A catalog record for this book is availabe from the Library of Congress

ISBN: 978-0-7506-8585-6

For information on all Architectural Press publications
visit our web site at books.elsevier.com

Printed and bound in Slovenia

08 09 10   10 9 8 7 6 5 4 3 2 1

Working together to grow
libraries in developing countries

www.elsevier.com | www.bookaid.org | www.sabre.org

ELSEVIER   **BOOK AID**
International   Sabre Foundation

Contents

Contents

Preface

In April 2004 Building Design began publishing working details from contemporary building projects that illustrate innovative construction techniques, forty of which are collated in this book. The projects have deliberately not been classified and appear in the order in which they were originally published. They exemplify the forefront of thinking in building technology yet also address timeless problems of architectural detailing.

The purpose of the details is not to provide ready-made solutions but to add to the resource base and stimulate thought. There are aspects of them all that can be criticised. Although the principles applied in solving different problems may be similar the final details are always specific to the conditions of the particular situation. The projects are presented here in the belief that by offering a tentative analogous solution that can then be criticised, we gain insight into our own problem and find fresh strands of thought to follow.

I would like to thank all the architects, engineers and photographers who have allowed their work to be reproduced in this book. (A full list of credits for each project is given before the index at the back of the book.) Thank you also to Robert Prewett for many stimulating conversations and to Emily Pitt for her inspiration, advice and support.

Why One Thing, not Another?

Georgian domestic architecture in Britain could be said to have evolved from the coincidence of a change in the law with a shift in tastes. Building legislation introduced in London and Westminster by acts of Parliament in 1707 and 1708 prohibited timber windows and doors from being placed closer than 4 inches from the face of a wall and stated that the front wall must be carried up 2½ feet above the garret floor and coped with stone.[1] Almost overnight the prevalent Dutch style of house with its flush windows and projecting timber cornice below the eaves was outlawed and a more austere way of building ushered in, where the masonry wall was left alone to define the architecture. Palladian classicism observed by travellers on the 'Grand Tour' in Italy was becoming de rigueur and the stripped down aesthetic fitted in well with the cultural mood. The new style was spread rapidly by pattern books that enabled builders anywhere to put up houses to a similar design.

Palladian classicism was in effect an abstract concept. Regulation and contextual circumstance determined how it would be applied in the particular context of the 18th Century. Architecture is a creative response to a particular set of constraints, an expression of the values of the people that made it. At the beginning of the 21st century there is a general agreement that we need to use resources more efficiently and make buildings more energy efficient. Legislation is affecting a significant shift in construction practice, although as yet no consensus has emerged as to how, or if, the means of achieving greater energy efficiency are expressed. The priorities of different designers are too varied for a single, epoch-defining style to prevail.

The lack of a dominant, recognised style is liberating but the multitude of parallel currents and movements exist in a vacuum of critical appraisal. Novelty or daring seems to buy immunity from criticism on more practical grounds. Ideas circulate in an amoral whirl of images and sound-bites ready to be applied to whatever brief is passing. If architects are to retain public confidence the relevance of ideas must be examined more closely. The choice of materials and the way they are assembled are not arbitrary. The designer is required to exercise value judgements, identifying what is required in a given situation and weighing up the likely effects of different choices.

So how do we make these choices? Why do we choose one thing over another?

Peter Salter has talked of the 'registration of circumstance'[2], the way a building might express the technical, cultural and perceptual conditions prevalent when it was constructed. The physical reality of the building, that is, what it is made of, how it is put together, how it sits in its surroundings is always seen through the perceptions of the users and the cultural climate in which it exists. A building's success as architecture will depend on how well these relationships have been judged.

In vernacular construction many of these decisions were already made. A house was built from the materials to hand, in ways evolved over generations. In a timber joint the actions of the maker are apparent, the marks of the tools attesting the human scale of the endeavour. We admire the unity of material, construction and form. The detailing and materials seem appropriate.

This measure of appropriateness seems to me what is often misjudged. There is no shortage of technical prowess for hire but there is a lack of control of how and when it is deployed. Just because something can be made to work does not mean it is necessarily desirable.

Timber window flush with brickwork of terraced houses at Newington Green, London built in 1658.

Timber window recessed from face of brickwork of Georgian terraced houses at Highbury Fields, London built in 1789.

Detailing, the act of drawing one component in relationship to another, forces us to consider how the elements of a building will work together, what effect one has on the others. The process informs the idea by testing it against practical issues and forcing it into a dialogue with other ideas with which it may not find harmony. An attitude to detailing develops through practice, evolving with each endeavour.

Appropriateness can be considered in relation to the architectural intent of the proposal, its context and implementation. What presence should it have? What do we want people to feel as they experience it? What mood does it communicate? How energy efficient does it need to be? Are the materials suitable for their tasks? How will it grow old? Who is going to make it? How will it be procured? Do the constraints of the project allow it?

The same questions should be in mind when looking at the projects in this book. In each case choices have been made, about which concerns are given priority and how they should be expressed. To understand these choices it is necessary to investigate the criteria on which they are based.

Procurement, labour and maintenance

Many buildings today are built using procurement routes where the architect's domain of influence is deliberately limited. Materials and details may have to be chosen shrewdly if they are to survive cost cutting or the passing of control to other hands.

Once the building is handed over to the client is anyone going to look after it? Feilden Clegg Bradley had to design their Westfield Student Village housing on the premise that the client didn't want to be burdened with a large, on-going maintenance cost. On the positive side, the client was persuaded to pay for higher-quality cladding materials, copper and hardwood, on the basis that they would weather and improve with age without needing to be re-sealed or painted.

The desire for a uniform, high level of craft was one of the aims of the Arts & Crafts movement. A uniform level is apparent on any building site in the UK but unfortunately it is not high. There are however some highly specialised subcontractors who are experts at particular forms of construction and it is to them we tend to turn if we want any guarantee of quality. Understanding what can be expected of the people who are going to make the different elements of the building informs how they are designed. There is no evidence that the situation has ever been much different. In the 18th Century, John Soane had his favourite London-based decorator whom he took to work on his country house projects to ensure that he got the quality of paintwork he demanded.

Environmental expression

Building regulations are being tightened to increase energy efficiency to the extent that conventional construction methods struggle to achieve the required standards. Many buildings which attempt to address energy conservation wear their hearts upon their sleeves, environmental expressionism as a badge of conscience. More compact products are evolving and architects are becoming more adept at integrating them into the building envelope. The crop store at the Renewable Energy Centre in Hertfordshire by Studio E Architects for example is built into an earth bank with an array of solar collectors as the waterproof layer on its sloping roof. The glass roof not only collects energy for the rest of the Centre but also traps heat to dry the biomass fuel stored beneath.

Conversely, a building with very high environmental credentials may not express them externally at all. The efficiency of solar collectors and wind

Solar panel roof of the crop store integrated with landscaping at the Renewable Energy Centre, Hertfordshire.

turbines has not quite reached a level where it makes economic sense to install them. It is important that the technology is pushed by demand but in terms of actual, immediate environmental benefit the best value for money is achieved through measures such as additional insulation, sourcing materials with low embodied energy, minimising air leakage and use of biomass fuel for space and water heating.

Regulations introduced in 2006 insist that buildings be proved to be air-tight. While reducing air leakage is essential the regulations do not deal sufficiently with vapour control. Almost all forms of construction currently rely on a vapour barrier near the inside of the envelope to prevent moisture penetrating into the walls or roof, condensing and causing growth of mould and rot. By making a building air- and vapour-tight it is essentially being wrapped up in a plastic bag. Trickle vents provide just enough air so the occupants do not suffocate but it is not a very healthy environment in which to live.

To ensure constant ventilation a whole house ventilation system can be installed with a heat exchanger to minimise heat losses. This could be a passive stack-effect system, which needs careful design and balancing to work efficiently, or a mechanical system. Humidity can be controlled by 'breathing walls' where the vapour barrier can be eliminated altogether by ensuring the construction becomes more vapour permeable towards the outside so vapour is naturally drawn out rather than trapped in the wall. ARC's House at Dalguise uses this principle in combination with an unfired clay brick inner leaf coated in 15-mm clay plaster which can also store moisture and reduce extremes of humidity. Analysis has found that relative humidity in the house remains roughly within the range of 40–60%, below the 60% level for dust mites to thrive and the 70% level required for mould growth.[3] The presence of dust mites and mould spores in the environment are known to trigger asthma and allergic reactions.

Materials, technology and practice

In spite of globalisation there are still vast regional differences in construction expertise. Architects working in an international domain have to identify the materials, techniques and skills available in the countries in which they are operating. Rem Koolhaas for example describes how he tries to 'use the specific virtues and qualities that can be achieved'[4] as a way of differentiating buildings in diverse locations.

In much of Europe concrete is the structural material of choice. In the 1970s steel became more popular in the UK but recently, huge demand for steel in China and an influx of affordable labour has made concrete construction affordable again for medium- and large-scale projects. Concrete incorporating a super-plasticising admixture, known as self-compacting concrete, is raising the standard of finish that can be expected and is allowing complex forms to be made more easily. At the City and County Museum in Lincoln, Panter Hudspith Architects specified such a mix to form a series of cranked, sloping roofs and to express the subtle relief of the formwork boards on the exposed walls. One wall in the café with several openings would have required seven separate pours to construct using conventional concrete. Using self-compacting concrete it was poured in one go.

There is growing expertise in timber construction in the UK because of its renewable credentials. Solid timber panels such as Merk's Lenotech system imported from Germany and constructed in the UK by Eurban combine sustainability, thermal mass, prefabrication and precision with real benefits of quality in the final product. Pringle Richards Sharratt used this system in their Carlisle Lane housing and the building shell was erected in 3 working days. Left exposed on the soffits, the panels can absorb moisture and store heat, reducing extremes of temperature and humidity.

The café wall with 7 openings built in one pour using self-compacting concrete at the City & County Museum, Lincoln.

A wall built using self-compacting concrete showing grain of timber shuttering and the impression of a leaf placed in the formwork at the City & County Museum, Lincoln.

Laminated timber is also being used in more complex structures. Grimshaw used Selective Laser Sintering to model and develop the roof of their Education Resource Centre for the Eden project. Computer numerically controlled (CNC) cutting machines were then used to manufacture the timber roof beams direct from the structural engineer's computer model without the need for translation into paper drawings. Such techniques allow incredible accuracy of fabrication, more than has ever been possible on site.

Perhaps a reason the construction industry has struggled to utilise mass production is that much research has aimed at achieving a complete product, a building that can be delivered in a finished state as a single component like an automobile. A building holds a responsibility to respond specifically to its context, unlike a car which celebrates its placelessness. The struggle to balance conflicting requirements is explicit in the best buildings. In the 1940s Alvar Aalto developed a system of prefabricated housing around the principle of 'flexible standardisation', where buildings might be made from a standard kit of parts of sufficient variety to produce a number of different types. The experiment lasted less than a decade and variety was generally minimised in other prefabricated systems to reduce labour costs. The provision for difference is something CNC machines can offer which may be the key to more mechanised construction methods.

Structure, Façade and Decoration

The Modernist preference for exposing structural elements is still manifest in many buildings today although structure is as often concealed as expressed and both strategies may be apparent in the same building. Most buildings in the UK are built with a framed structure. The outer skin has been detached from the structure so that the construction of the building is no longer necessarily expressed in its external skin. The architect is forced to take a position on the play between the language of structure and the language of skin.

At one end of the spectrum the Alpine House at Kew Gardens by Wilkinson Eyre has a completely exposed structure in the tradition of the Victorian glass house. The auditorium at Kingsdale School by DeRijke Marsh Morgan on the other hand has a beautiful structural skeleton of timber poles that is completely concealed by plywood panels.

A hybrid approach was taken by Keith Williams Architects at the Unicorn Theatre. Two solid volumes cantilever out over the foyer with no visible means of support other than a thin glass curtain wall. The weight of the volumes is implicit in their size, but the external walls are rendered or clad in copper concealing the reinforced concrete and steel structure behind. The render, copper and glass are all of a similar thickness. The external expression of the building is a play between the transparency, reflectance and texture of the different surface layers.

The façade is the site of the most apparent experimentation in recent architecture, partly perhaps because it is often the only part of the building on which the architect is given free reign. Rational expression of structure is hard to reconcile with the demand for speedy, low-cost construction. For some clients the façade treatment is the only added value they perceive they will gain from an architect's involvement. The obsession with the external appearance of buildings means materials are often chosen for their appearance alone rather than their appropriateness.

Building skins are becoming increasingly complex to help regulate the environment inside. BBC Broadcasting House by MacCormac Jamieson Prichard and the Centre for Nanotechnology by Feilden Clegg Bradley have multiple layered façades incorporating gantries for cleaning and maintenance as well as different types of glass and screens to control daylight, views

5-axis CNC cutter forming the timber roof members of the Education Resource Centre for the Eden Project, Cornwall.

Computer rendering showing concrete and steel structure of the Unicorn Theatre, London, concealed by cladding in the finished building.

Reflections and Interference patterns on the façade of the Centre for Nanotechnology, UCL, London.

Whole brick reveal at front door and internal window linings expressing the thickness of the wall of house at Newington Green, London.

and sun penetration. The way the layers overlay and reflect one another generates patterns of transparency and opaqueness, light and shade, an order not dissimilar to a classical rhythm. The effect these patterns create is something beyond what is strictly necessary for the performance of the façade. The moiré effect caused by interference between the two layers of the façade of the Centre for Nanotechnology is purely decorative, a kind of virtual ornament.

Clad buildings can only achieve depth by layering several materials over one another in this way or by contriving a thickening of the skin. Monolithic buildings have a tangible mass that can be expressed and appropriate materials can be used through the thickness of the wall for different functions. There may be plaster on the inside or better quality bricks on the outer face than in the centre. A wall could be seen as having two façades, one internal and one external relating to completely different users, atmospheres and environmental conditions.

For the house at Newington Green that my practice designed, we deliberately tried to express these qualities. It is built of a single material, brick, very close to the street at the end of a Victorian terrace. A different brick is used for the inner and outer leafs of the cavity walls because the inner leaf requires a higher compressive strength to carry the floors and roof. The bricks are painted matt white inside giving a soft background texture to the interior. The white paint disguises the difference between the interior brick and the face brick but the textures are different and both are laid in stretcher bond so it is obvious to the trained eye that it is a cavity wall. Externally the windows are flush with the bricks but the front door is recessed with a whole brick reveal, inviting the visitor across the threshold. Of course we agonised over all these issues but in the end we tried to express the characteristics that were appropriate to the atmosphere we were trying to create.

Effect

This desire to create an effect hits at the root of the role of detailing. Architects make choices of which things are seen and which are not, what is exaggerated and what is played down based on what effect they are trying to achieve. Creating a particular atmosphere, mood or emotional response is in the end the point of architecture, the intent that raises it above mere building. The choices required to achieve the desired effect may well run contrary to concepts such as honesty or allegiance of form and function.

The soffit of the cloister at the Novy Dvur Monastery by John Pawson Architects is made of curved plasterboard on a standard suspended ceiling system. Hardly the sort of material that sent Le Corbusier into raptures as he walked around Le Thoronet but it is out of reach overhead and detailed with such skill and in a way that appears solid. Using plasterboard was a choice that enabled the effect to be achieved within the budget. The vault may in fact have been impossible to achieve in say concrete without additional structural support. A rationalist might say that the building has been demeaned by using a lightweight, thin material like plasterboard where weight might be expected. It could also be argued that if you do not perceive it, it does not matter.

The atmosphere of a space is determined by the physical properties and the sensory presence of the materials from which it is formed. It bears the character of the processes by which it was made and the way the construction was conceived in the mind of the designer. For me a knowledge of the specific circumstances of how a project will be realised is fundamental in the conception of the intent. Only through a deep understanding of materials and construction can the connection be made between intent and physical form.

References

1. From Covent Garden 'The Bedford Estate: From 1700 to 1802', *Survey of London*, Volume 36, 1970, pp. 37–40.

2. See Peter Salter's Introduction to *Brick-Work: Thinking and Making*, gta/ ETH, Zurich, October 2005.

3. See 'Feat of Clay' by Tom Morton in *Materials World*, pp. 23–24, January 2006 and the research on ARC's website at http://www.arc-architects.com

4. Rem Koolhaas – Interview with the author, Porto, 3 April 2005.

Photo credit: Jason Lowe

Photo credit: Jason Lowe

Photo credit: Muf

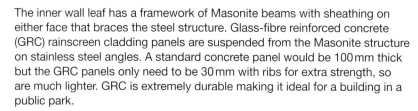

Photo credit: Muf

Photo credit: Muf

Photo credit: Muf

Verulamium Hypocaust Building, St Albans

Architect: muf architecture/art
Consulting Engineer: Atelier One

In the 1920s a well-preserved mosaic floor was uncovered during excavations of the Roman city of Verulamium in modern day St Albans. Playing fields were laid over the archaeological area to protect it and the mosaic was left exposed in a drab utilitarian brick building. In 1999 muf won a competition to replace it with a new structure.

Disturbance of the ground has been minimised by using 24 micro-piles, threaded perforated steel tubes 3 cm in diameter which are drilled into the earth and pumped with grout. The galvanised steel frame is fixed to the piles via circular concrete pile caps. Gabions filled with flints form a continuous wall retaining the earth around the building's perimeter.

The inner wall leaf has a framework of Masonite beams with sheathing on either face that braces the steel structure. Glass-fibre reinforced concrete (GRC) rainscreen cladding panels are suspended from the Masonite structure on stainless steel angles. A standard concrete panel would be 100 mm thick but the GRC panels only need to be 30 mm with ribs for extra strength, so are much lighter. GRC is extremely durable making it ideal for a building in a public park.

Eighty-six 1.6 m wide panels were pre-fabricated in different shapes to follow the slope of the ground. Finely crushed oyster shells were used as aggregate in the concrete, a common practice in ancient Rome, and more shells were rolled into the surface before the concrete had cured in the mould. The shells give the exterior a pearlescent shine and provide a rough surface to deter climbing and graffiti. Shaped rubber forms were placed in the concrete moulds to make the rosette windows.

At either end the roof kicks up to allow light in through a glazed clerestory strip. The glazing is frameless with a single laminated pane spanning from wall to roof and the roof provides no structural restraint to the top of the wall. On the elevation facing the town there is no steel in the wall so the timber structure acts as a cantilever with a full moment connection to the steel beam at its base which makes it rigid. Mirrored acrylic is fixed to the soffit on the approach side to give glimpses of the mosaic to approaching visitors and allow people inside an inverted reflection of the town.

Site plan, scale 1:5000

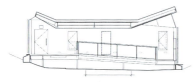

Section, scale 1:300

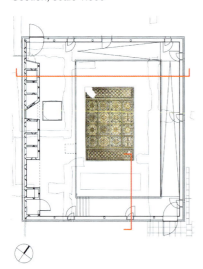

Plan with section and area of detail shown in red, scale 1:300

1. Roof
Sedum planting in 80 mm soil.
Drainage mat.
80 mm extruded polystyrene insulation.
Bituminous felt waterproof membrane.
18 mm WBP plywood roof deck.
200 × 50 mm softwood roof joists on galvanised hangers.
Steel frame primary roof structure.
Ceiling void.
2 layers plasterboard suspended ceiling.
Acrylic mirror glued to underside of plasterboard.

2. Roof ridge
PPC aluminium fascia.
Polished stainless steel mirrored soffit.

3. High level windows
Steel channel at head fixed to timber joists to allow for +/−5 mm roof deflection.
Single laminated glazing in 1200 mm widths.
Aluminium channel section at bottom fixed to timber structure.

4. Top of wall
Aluminium flashing dressed down into gutter.
Aluminium gutter.

5. External wall
Glass fibre reinforced concrete (GFRC) rainscreen cladding panels with oyster shell inlays and rosette-shaped cut outs.
Stainless steel shelf angles with dowels to locate cladding panels bolted to timber frame.
Nominal 75 mm ventilation gap.
Breather membrane.
18 mm OSB external sheathing.
200 mm Masonite beam structural framework to inner leaf fixed to steel frame.

200 mm blown cellulose fibre insulation.
12 mm plywood inner sheathing.
25 mm softwood battens.
12 mm birch faced plywood lining.

6. Windows
Rosette cut-out in external cladding panel.
External steel framed double glazed inward opening window.
Internal frameless single glazed opening window held on patch plates. Glass fritted from transparent behind rosette openings to opaque behind solid wall.
Birch faced plywood window lining.

7. Walkway
Precast concrete slabs bolted to steelwork.
Steel balustrade uprights made from 2 × 20 mm thick flats bolted to 20 mm steel plate bracket below through notches in precast slabs.
60 mm diameter stainless steel handrail.

8. External wall/ground junction
130 × 4 mm stainless steel plate fascia skirting.
Galvanised steel perimeter cavity closer.
Geotextile drainage membrane.
50 mm rigid polystyrene insulation board.
Flint filled gabion retaining wall.
Soil reinforcement around perimeter.

9. Foundations
450 mm diameter concrete pile caps.
Micropiles injected with grout.

10. Floor
Original Roman mosaic floor on tile pillar hypocaust.

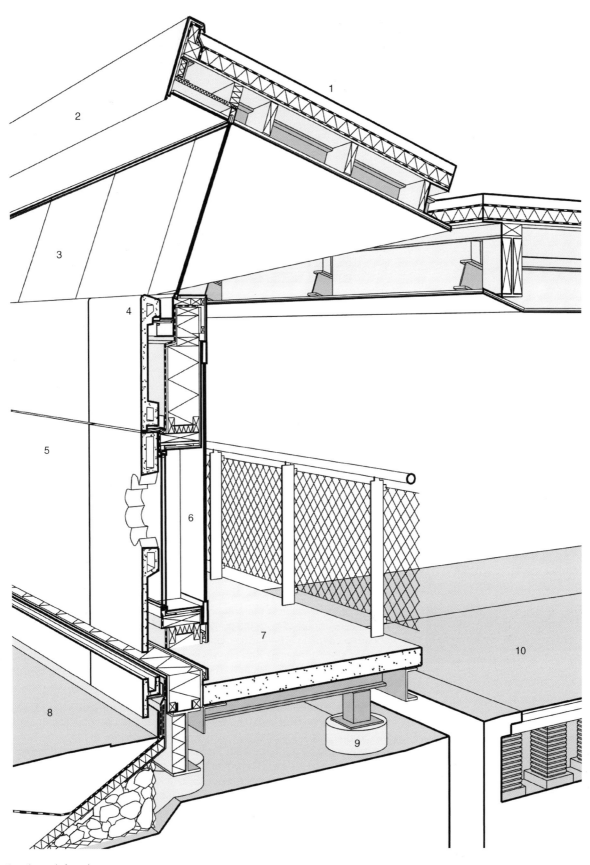

Section through façade

Bedford School Library, Bedford

Architect: Eric Parry Architects
Structural Engineer: Adams Kara Taylor

Bedford School is an independent boys' school catering for day pupils and boarders aged seven to eighteen. In 2001 Eric Parry Architects won a competition to design a new library at the school. The library has a curved brick upper storey with a barrel vault roof. A long window at ground floor looks out on playing fields.

Deep mass concrete strip foundations support load-bearing masonry ground floor walls and the beam-and-block ground floor itself. The external walls above first floor level step out supported on a pre-cast concrete ledge element that transfers the load back to the ground floor blockwork. The first floor is a concrete slab cast directly onto the ledge counterbalancing the weight of the wall. Over the ground floor entrance and window the ledge is entirely supported from the mezzanine, which is in turn supported on concrete columns. The 215 mm brickwork wall wraps around the building in a continuous 56 m sweep with curved specials used to create the sinuous form. The whole-brick thickness and lime mortar specially tested by the BRE for strength allow movement joints to be eliminated.

The roof is a barrel vault in section, extruded around the building to follow the curving perimeter wall. The wall was intended to carry the roof directly but the programme implications of allowing the lime mortar to fully cure before the roof could be started meant that steel posts had to be introduced to carry the primary roof steels. The roof and walls could then be built simultaneously. A series of curved universal beam (UB) sections form the vault, tied together with circular hollow section (CHS) purlins, some of which are curved twice in their length. Timber rafters are bolted to plates welded to the purlins. Each timber has been individually drawn and cut from a 250 × 50 mm joist to a unique curved profile. It was proposed to use a computer-controlled cutter but the contractor chose to cut each rafter by hand. The roof finish is pre-patinated zinc with single-ply membrane gutters and flat areas.

Photo credit: Peter Cook

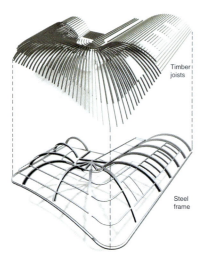

Exploded diagram of roof structure

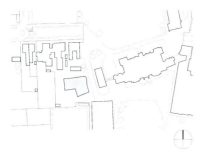

Site plan, scale 1:4000

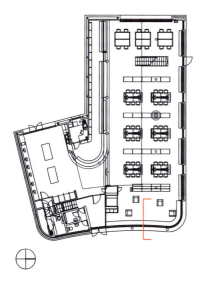

Ground floor plan, scale 1:500

1. Foundations
2 m deep mass concrete footings.
215 mm hollow blockwork wall slotted over reinforcement and filled with concrete.
Mass concrete upstand.
Liquid applied tanking membrane to all faces of concrete cill.
Sheet bituminous tanking membrane to outer face of mass concrete.
Sheet bituminous tanking membrane wrapped around beam ends and up to underside of timber cill.

2. Ground floor
17 mm reclaimed iroko boards glued to screed.
80 mm reinforced sand-cement screed over low temperature underfloor heating pipes.
30 mm rigid perimeter insulation.
50 mm rigid insulation.
Polythene vapour barrier.
Beam and block floor structure.
Ventilated cavity.

3. Mezzanine floor
Carpet finish.
20 mm tongued & grooved chipboard.
Underfloor heating pipes with metal plate heat sink set into insulation.
25 mm acoustic and thermal insulation.
275 mm concrete slab.
Painted plaster soffit.

4. Mezzanine Steelwork
200 × 100 mm PFC (parallel flange channel) eaves tie beam providing restraint to external brickwork.
200 x 200 mm SHS (square hollow section) posts bolted to mezzanine slab.

5. Mezzanine slab edge
Precast concrete structural ledge lintel.
275 mm thick concrete mezzanine slab cast over ledge lintel.
Flexible cavity tray over lintel.

6. External wall
215 mm class B wirecut facing brick outer leaf.
Mortar 3:1 sharp sand:lime with no vertical movement joints.
Cavity with 50 mm rigid insulation.
Concrete blockwork inner leaf.
Painted plaster finish.

7. Roof structure
Curved UBs (universal beam) with rigid plate connections to vertical SHS posts.
Curved CHS (circular hollow section) purlins bolted to primary UBs.
Mild steel plates welded to CHS.
Curved timber joists cut from 250 × 50 C24 joists (max. 600 c/c) bolted to plates.

8. Parapet and gutter
PPC metal coping.
Vertical single ply membrane to top of parapet.
Single ply membrane gutter lining.
WBP plywood gutter on softwood frame.
Single ply membrane on softwood boards over vaulted area.

9. Ceiling
Three coats plaster on metal lath wired to bearers.
12 mm diameter galvanised mild steel bearers suspended from joists on galvanised straps.
Vapour barrier.
125 mm mineral wool insulation.

10. Vaulted roof areas
0.7 mm standing seam pre-weathered zinc.
100 × 20 mm softwood boards 2-3 mm apart.
50 mm ventilation gap.
High grade building paper roof underlay.

11. Stepped eaves
1 mm pre-weathered zinc eaves fascia.
Insect mesh over ventilation slot.
Single ply upstand.

12. Built-in seating
Painted MDF bench with slots over heater.
Finned tube radiator curved to follow curve of window and seat.
Skirting slot in seat for air inlet.

13. Window
Iroko frame with curved 12 mm toughened glass at corner.
Concrete columns supporting mezzanine slab.
In-situ reinforced concrete cill.
Cobbles set in mortar to protect window and avoid need for manifestation.

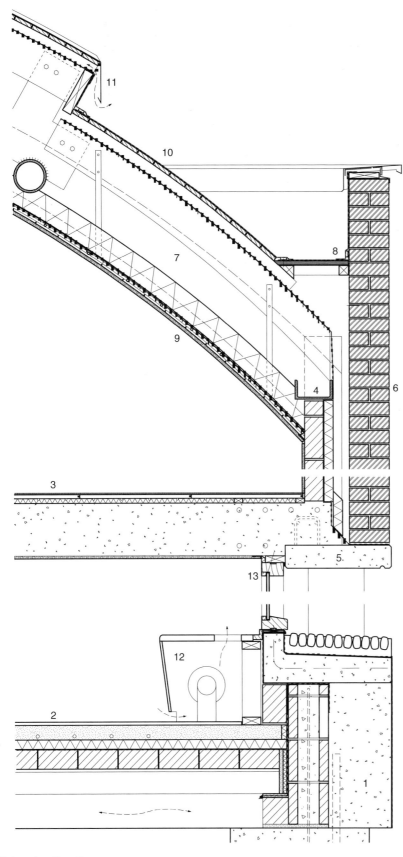

External wall section

Digital Studio at Oxford Brookes School of Architecture, Oxford

Architect: Niall McLaughlin Architects
Desk Fabricator: Isis Concepts Ltd

Photo credit: Nicholas Kane

This design studio occupies the top floor of a 1960s concrete framed building. It is a big room – 30 m long with a 3.6 m floor to ceiling height. The concrete surfaces were causing sound to reverberate around making private conversation impossible. To counteract the resonance of the hard surfaces a series of profiled Melatech foam sound absorbing baffles have been suspended on isolating hangers from the ceiling.

Four cable trays running the length of the studio contain fluorescent batten light fittings. Power and data cables are threaded through wire eyelet guides and dropped down to new workstations below in bright yellow air-line conduits. Purpose-made wire coat hangers hook over the cable tray.

The workstations themselves have a steel carcass. A plinth is formed from 50 × 25 mm box sections electro-resistance welded to minimise distortion and mounted on a 10 mm thick base plate. The plinth is clad in 1.2 mm gauge folded steel with a lockable door where a computer can be stored. The desktop is designed to take the weight of a person standing on the end of the 800 mm cantilever. The fabricator worked hard to reduce the thickness to only 41 mm. An 18 mm MDF top is stiffened by a framework of paired 20 × 10 mm steel box sections welded to very tight tolerances. The outer faces are clad with steel panels.

Two-thirds of the desktop is an opening lid on concealed Soss hinges with two 700 Newton gas struts to aid movement. The lid conceals a cable and storage tray. The inner desk surface is finished with laminate and the inside of the lid has a steel panel where drawings can be magnetically pinned up. The lid is formed from welded 20 × 10 mm box sections with rigid polystyrene infill to reduce local deformation. All the steel panels are nylon powder coated (NPC), which is eight to ten times more durable than polyester powder coating.

Photo credit: Nicholas Kane

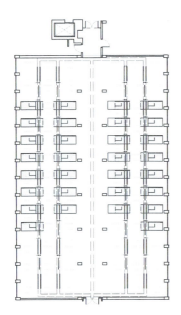

Floor plan, scale 1:400

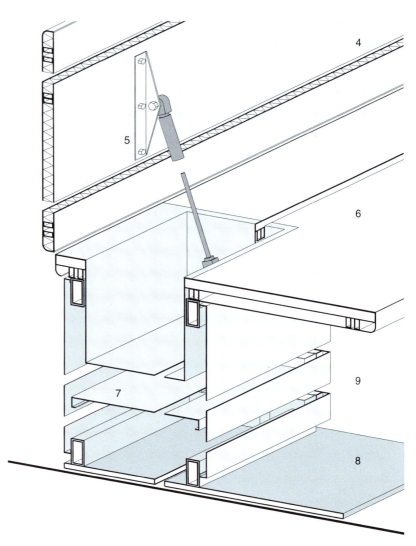

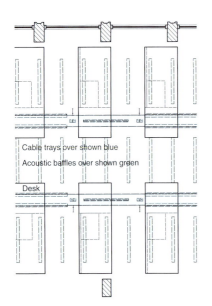

Cable trays over shown blue
Acoustic baffles over shown green

Desk

Typical bay plan with reflected ceiling
services, scale 1:100

Section through workstation

1. Ceiling
Existing concrete soffit made good and painted
with matt emulsion.

2. Acoustic baffles
1200 × 600 × 75mm baffle custom cut from
Melatech foam.
Class 1 fire rated wire-isolating hangers fixed
into concrete soffit with expanding anchor
bolts.

3. Cable tray
300mm wide perforated galvanised steel cable
tray.
Galvanised hanger rods fixed to concrete soffit
with expanding anchor bolts.
Paired 1500mm long fluorescent battens with
cool white lamps mounted so that only lamps
are visible from below.
Single 1200mm long fluorescent battens with
ultra-violet lamps to up-light soffit.
Galvanised steel bent 4mm rod with mounting
plate fixed inside cable tray to guide cables
from desks.

Power and data sockets mounted inside cable
tray.

4. Desk lid
2.0mm gauge nylon powder coated (NPC) steel
casing.
20 × 10mm paired steel box section frame
electro-resistance welded.
20mm thick extruded polystyrene infill between
box sections.
1.2mm gauge nylon powder coated steel inner
panel.

5. Opening mechanism
Two 700 Newton gas struts bolted through steel
panels back to frame.
Five Soss hinges screwed to metal brackets
welded to steel box section frames.

6. Inner desktop
1.6mm laminate surface.
Inset folded nylon powder coated steel storage
tray with cable outlet.
18mm MDF base.

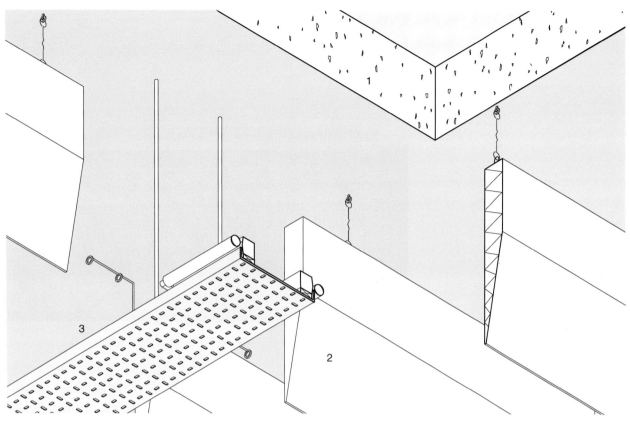

Section through ceiling

20 × 10 mm paired steel box section frame electro-resistance welded.
1.5 mm gauge nylon powder coated steel under-panel.

7. Plinth
1.2 mm gauge nylon powder coated steel outer cladding panels.
Lockable door formed from 1.2 mm gauge nylon powder coated steel sheet.
Shelf for computer formed from 1.2 mm gauge nylon powder coated steel sheet.

Structure formed from electro-resistance welded 50 × 25 mm steel box section.

8. Base
800 × 800 × 10 mm thick nylon powder coated steel base plate on rubber feet.

9. Floor
2.5 mm linoleum glued to prepared concrete slab.

Photo credit: Hertha Hurnaus

Trevision Production Building
Vienna, Austria

Architects: Querkraft Architekten

Photo credit: Querkraft Architekten

Photo credit: Querkraft Architekten

Trevision manufacture large-scale banners for advertising and cultural events. For its new production facility near Vienna, Querkraft have used two of these banners to define the building's main elevations. Facing the autobahn to the north a backlit translucent screen has been printed with a mountain panorama. To the south a PVC net printed with the word 'unvorbeischaubar' ('unoverlookable') prevents overlooking from the surrounding landscape while from inside the text is only visible obliquely so does not impede the view out. The banners are held in tension by aluminium frames fixed back to a steel structure.

Entry to the building is via a cantilevered walkway on the south side that also provides solar shading to the offices and a canopy to the loading area. Tapered steel T-section beams carry a galvanised steel grating deck and a thin steel balustrade.

Foundations are 1 m deep ground beams on recycled concrete hardcore. The mezzanine office area has a concrete floor and structure to provide one and a half hours' fire protection. The rest of the structure is steel on a 6.2 m grid. The structural grid was determined by the spans of standard cladding panels to eliminate the need for secondary steelwork. The cladding panels are butt jointed without cover strips and glazing units are set in 20 mm deep aluminium channels and silicone jointed to the panels.

The roof is a profiled galvanised steel deck exposed on the underside. Cut-to-falls insulation takes rainwater to syphonic outlets in the single-ply membrane waterproof layer. The building is naturally ventilated with opening aluminium windows and rooflights.

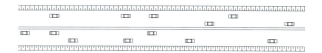

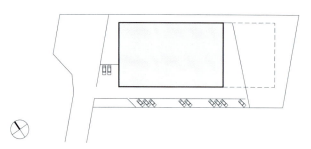

Site plan, scale 1:2000

Section, scale 1:750

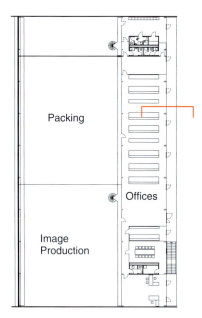

First floor plan, scale 1:750

1. Façade lights
Floodlights fixed to tapering 250 × 120 steel T-section fixed back to perimeter stub beams.

2. Roof
Single-ply UPVC waterproof membrane.
100–200 mm rigid thermal insulation cut to falls.
Vapour barrier.
150 mm deep profiled galvanised steel roof deck.
Rainwater pipe connected to syphonic outlets varies from 50 to 110 mm diameter.

3. Roof perimeter
Single-ply UPVC waterproof membrane.
18 mm chipboard deck.
160 × 80 mm RHS (rectangular hollow section) steel eaves tie beam.
150 mm deep profiled galvanised steel roof deck.
300 × 390 mm deep tapering T-section steel stub beams.

4. Printed screen
PVC net held in tension between extruded aluminium frames top and bottom.
Net printed with text externally.

5. External walkway
Tapering 200 × 260 mm deep steel stub beams bolted back to concrete frame.
260 × 90 mm PFC steel edge beam.
100 × 100 mm steel I-section joists at 1035 mm centres.
40 mm deep galvanised steel grating.

6. Balustrade
Mild steel angle handrail.
Mild steel flat uprights.
Steel cable balustrades.

7. Glazing
2960 × 1300 mm sealed double-glazed units.

Proprietary aluminium frame at bottom.
20 mm deep aluminium channel at head.
Silicone joints at glass-to-glass joints and to steel.
Aluminium framed doors.

8. Steel frame
340 × 330 mm steel I-section columns bolted to first floor slab.
300 × 390 mm deep steel I-section beams at 6200 mm centres.
300 × 150 mm deep T-section tie beam formed by cutting I-section in half.
89 × 10 mm CHS cross-bracing in two bays.

9. First floor
Carpet finish.
600 × 600 mm proprietary raised floor on adjustable pedestals.
160 mm services void.
200 mm deep reinforced concrete floor slab.

10. External wall
1100 mm wide × 120 mm thick aluminium-faced insulated cladding panels.
One double-glazed aluminium framed opening window per bay.

11. Concrete frame
400 × 500 mm deep reinforced concrete columns and beams at 6200 mm centres.

12. Ground floor
4 mm PVC flooring.
150 mm floating reinforced concrete slab.
Recycled concrete hardcore.

13. Foundations
1000 mm deep ground beams.
80 mm thick rigid perimeter insulation.

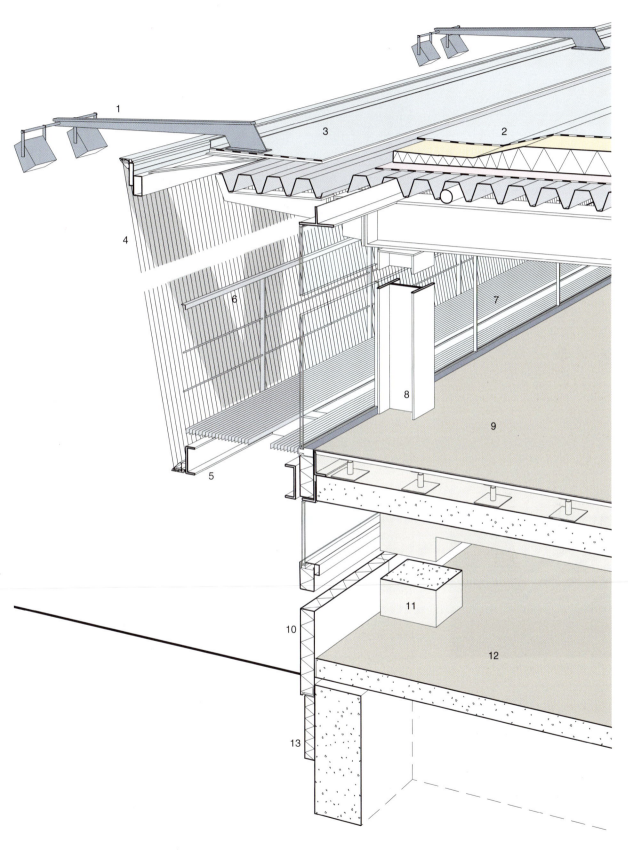

Section through south façade

Photo credit: courtesy of Studio E Architects Ltd

Crop Store,
Renewable Energy Centre
Kings Langley, Hertfordshire

Architects: Studio E Architects
M & E Services Engineer: Max Fordham & Partners

Photo credit: courtesy of Studio E Architects Ltd

Photo credit: courtesy of RES/Fusion

Renewable Energy Systems, an international wind energy company, have converted a former chicken farm into 2700 square metres of office space. Thanks to a €400,000 EC grant the project was carried out as a demonstration of zero-carbon building technologies.

The existing building was largely rebuilt using materials with low embodied energies to optimise natural ventilation, daylight, high insulation, low air-infiltration and solar control. A 225 kW wind turbine can deliver all the site's energy needs with enough spare capacity to power about 40 homes.

Bales of Miscanthus, used as fuel for a 100 kW biomass boiler are stacked in the crop store. The end walls of the building are formed from galvanised steel mesh to allow air to blow through and dry out the crop. To minimise impact on its greenbelt location the building is set into the ground. Gabions filled with stone retain the earth and form the exposed internal walls of the store. A geotextile membrane is laid over the outside of the gabions to prevent groundwater ingress.

The floor is a concrete raft slab and a steel frame supports the roof, independent of the gabion walls. The roof has a continuous one metre strip of aluminium framed skylights, but is predominantly clad with solar panels. There are twenty-two 4.2 × 1.7 metre thermal panels, seven of which also have a photovoltaic (PVT) array which converts light from the sun directly into electricity at about 15% efficiency. The thermal collectors have a black painted copper plate which absorbs the sun's heat and transmits it to water in copper pipes welded to the back of the plate at about 70°C.

Photo credit: courtesy of RES/Fusion

An 1100 square metre water tank stores the heat. It has a 500 mm thick floating polystyrene lid and a two metre thick mixture of chalk and clay around the perimeter as an insulator to keep the water in the store at between 20 and 50°C. During the winter hot water will be taken from the heat store to preheat the fresh air supply to the building.

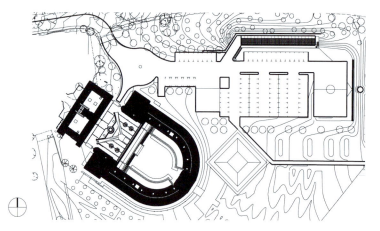

Site plan, scale 1:2000

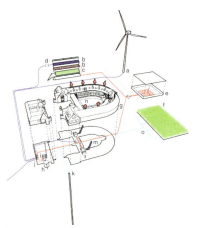

a. 225kw Wind Turbine
b. Hybrid PVT Array
c. Crop Store
d. PV Invertors
e. 1500m3 Water Heat Sink
f. Biomass Crop (Miscanthus)
g. Renewable Energy Centre
h. Crop Shredder
i. Biomass Boilers &
   Gas Fired Backup Boilers
j. Electrical Import/Exort Meters
k. 80m Deep Borehole in Chalk Aquifer
l. 2No. Air Handling Installations
m. Fresh Air
n. Exhaust Air
o. Irrigation

Energy strategy diagram

1. Roof ridge
100 × 100 mm vertical treated softwood studs at 500 mm centres fixed to steel channel.
19 mm WBP plywood upstand.
2 mm thick mill finish aluminium capping mechanically fixed with self-tapping screws on back leg.
Continuous adhesive faced butyl sealant strip between capping and glazing head section.

2. Rooflights
Continuous strip of 990 × 990 mm aluminium framed roof lights with 6 mm laminated glass.

3. Flashings
2 mm thick mill finish aluminium flashing.

4. Solar Panel
4276 × 1776 mm mill finished aluminium frame.
6 mm laminated glass outer pane.
Air gap.
Black painted copper plate with water filled copper pipes welded to back and photovoltaic receptors bonded to front face.
Rigid insulation behind copper pipes.

5. Roof secondary structure
50 × 50 mm treated softwood battens at 600 mm centres to support solar panels.
0.25 micron polythene sheet.
19 mm WBP plywood.
200 × 50 mm treated softwood joists spanning between steels at 600 centres.
50 × 50 mm treated softwood batten beneath joists on steel flanges.

6. Front Gutter
Flat 2 mm thick mill finish aluminium gutter on 19 mm WBP plywood on 100 × 100 mm treated softwood bearers at 500 mm centres.
19 mm WBP plywood upstand nailed to continuous 200 × 38 mm softwood treated timber nailed to end of 100 × 100 mm bearers.

Continuous treated softwood packing to suit uneven top edge of gabions.

7. Rear Gutter
100 mm depth fine stone aggregate ballast.
Single layer mineral felt on building paper separating layer.
400 mm wide continuous strip of geotextile membrane dressed up face of edge trim.
25 mm WBP birch faced plywood.
100 × 50 mm treated softwood battens at 1000 mm centres.
145 × 21 mm softwood edge trim secured to 100 mm long 25 × 50 mm softwood treated battens at 500 mm centres.

8. Gabion retaining walls
Stone filled galvanised steel gabion cages.
0.25 micron polythene carried vertically to protect timber against ground moisture and dressed over top of gabion overlaid and protected by geotextile membrane.

9. Steel Frame
152 × 152 mm galvanised UC (Universal Column) front posts at 7200 mm centres.
203 × 203 mm galvanised UC rear posts at 7200 mm centres.
352 × 172 mm galvanised UB (Universal Beam) tie at front and rear.
254 × 146 mm galvanised UB roof beams at 3600 mm centres.

10. Floor slab
200 mm reinforced concrete slab increasing to 450 mm at edges.
Damp proof membrane.
50 mm sand blinding on 150 mm hardcore.
Edge strips between slab and gabions filled with gravel to form water soak-away.

11. Pipework
Circulation pipework to solar panels.

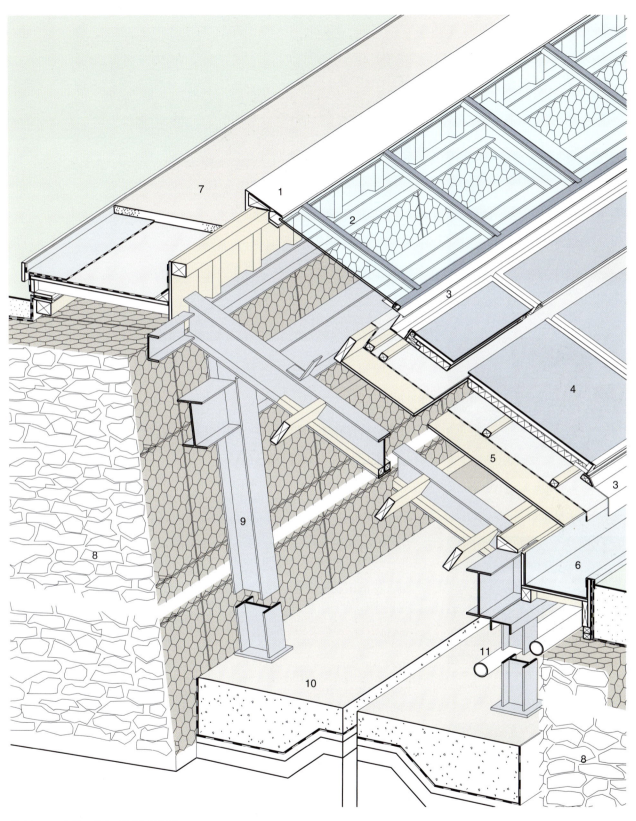

Cut-away section through crop store

Fountain on the Nikolaikirchhof Leipzig, Germany

Architects: David Chipperfield Architects

The Nikolaikirchhof is a public space with historical significance both in the medieval structure of Leipzig and in the events leading up to the reunification of Germany. It is paved with artificial cobbles made in the late nineteenth century from copper smelting slag. Relieved of the duty of a public water point, the fountain achieves a presence by its materiality of water and stone. Its low form is a counterpoint to a column monument at the other end of the space.

The 3.5 m diameter bowl of the fountain consists of a single monolithic piece of Saxonian granite, the same stone as the pavements around the Nikolaikirchhof. Various quarries were considered before one was found with sufficient bed depth to produce the required size. Once excavated, a timber shelter was erected around the 60 tonne stone and the bowl was hand cut in the quarry by two masons. The carved bowl, reduced to a weight of 17 tonnes, could then be craned on to a transporter and taken to site.

Water flows over the rim equally in all directions requiring the bowl to sit perfectly level. It was supported at three points using inflatable air cushions which allow very accurate height adjustment. Once level, concrete was pumped in under the bowl as a permanent base. Final adjustments were made by taking up to 2 mm off the rim before completion. A further 2 mm has been allowed for future removal in case of settlement but this has so far been unnecessary.

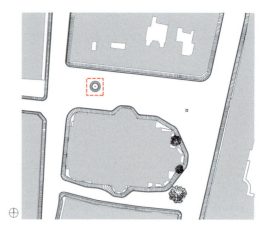

Site plan, scale 1:2000

A plinth of granite stones encircles the fountain with an inward fall. Water trickling down the rough outer face of the bowl drains back through a 20 mm slot to a concealed continuous prefabricated stainless steel gutter. A plant room beneath contains pumping equipment with access via a stainless steel trap door clad with the same granite as the fountain.

1. Stone bowl
3300 mm diameter × 1135 mm deep Lausitz granite bowl hand-cut to shape in the quarry.
Smooth finished internal surface.
Rough cut external surface.
Central hole for water supply pipe with stainless steel cover.

2. Stone plinth
20 mm continuous drainage slot between bowl and plinth.
1300 mm deep × 320 mm thick tapered Lausitz granite plinth stones laid to falls to lap beneath bowl.
10 mm joints between stones pointed with mortar.
50 mm mortar bed.
Mass concrete base cast to falls.

3. Gutter
300 mm wide prefabricated stainless steel secret gutter fixed to stone bowl.
Four gulley outlets welded into gutter.

4. Paving
Original 150 × 150 mm cobbles made from copper smelting slag relayed around fountain.

40 mm sand blinding.
200 mm gravel base.
Compacted hardcore.

5. Access door
1100 × 1100 mm stainless steel access door with gas-strut opening mechanism.
1100 × 1100 × 70 mm thick granite slab to conceal metal door.
Stainless steel frame cast into concrete base.

6. External wall of plant room
300 mm thick waterproof concrete wall.
Permanent timber framework supporting steel shutter.

7. Floor of plant room
Minimum thickness 50 mm sand–cement screed laid to falls.
100 × 50 mm drainage channel in screed.
300 mm thick waterproof concrete floor.
600 × 600 × 600 mm sump beneath pump.
100 mm gravel blinding.

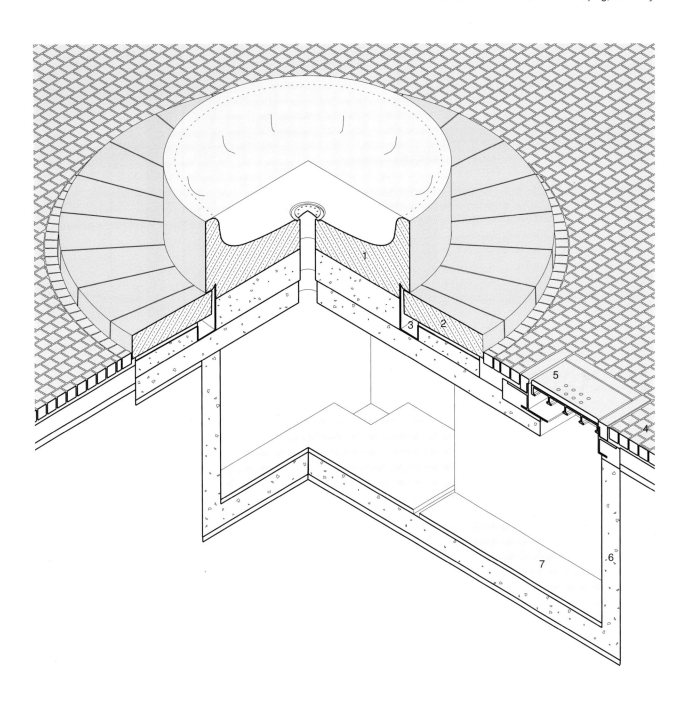

Cut-away section through fountain

Photo credit: Jonathan Lovekin

Youl Hwa Dang Publishing House
Paju Book City, Seoul, South Korea

Architect: Architecture Research Unit (ARU)
Local Architect: Metropolitan Architecture Research Unit (MARU)

Photo credit: Kang Kyoung Hwa, MARU

Photo credit: Philip Christou, ARU

The idea behind Paju Book City is to bring together the previously dispersed South Korean publishing industry in a planned estate near Seoul. Under a framework plan by Florian Beigel's Architecture Research Unit it is hoped that 300 different publishing and media companies will commission their own buildings and relocate there. One of the first to be built is the headquarters of the Youl Hwa Dang Publishing House.

The four-storey concrete framed building sits on a concrete basement undercroft used as a car park. Piled foundations suspend the building at an artificial ground level in a reclaimed wetland site. The perimeter elevations are clad in a timber rainscreen whilst the elevations inside the site boundary are translucent.

The translucent façades have a secondary structure of steel angles spanning between the concrete columns. A lattice of 60 × 60 mm square hollow sections provides intermediate support. All steel connections have been site welded to give fine tolerances. Externally the façade appears as a series of thin metal shelves supporting the glazing. Purpose-made powder coated aluminium angles cover the steel angle and hold the glazing in place. The outer glazing is 8 mm toughened cast glass with a ripple pattern making it slightly opaque. Setting the glass at a 3–4 degree angle breaks down the idea of the façade as a plane and emphasises the shelf angles. An inner skin of three-wall polycarbonate is held in aluminium frames fixed back to the steel. The aluminium glazing angles are set on 6 mm rubber spacers. Both the spacers and the rear glazing locators have intermittent gaps to allow air to circulate in the cavity, removing heat built up behind the glass.

Photo credit: Jonathan Lovekin

The timber rainscreen façades have E-section galvanised steel studs spanning from floor to ceiling, dry-lined with plasterboard internally. 12 mm plywood sheathing is fixed to the outer face of the studs with 100 mm of foil-backed rigid insulation in between. Black stained cedar boards are fixed to timber battens over a breather membrane to form the rainscreen. Thick insulation compensates for the lower thermal performance of the translucent façades.

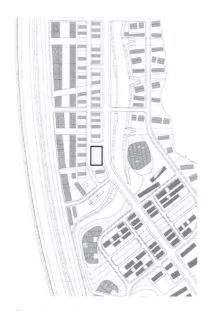

Site plan, scale 1:10000

Ground floor plan, scale 1:750

Section, scale 1:750

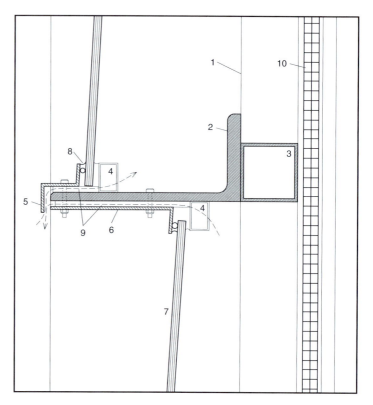

Detail section through glazing support shelf, scale 1:5

1. Secondary structure
Line of 100 × 100 × 6 × 8 mm structural steel
I-section column beyond.

2. Shelf Angle
200 × 90 × 9 × 14 mm unequal steel shelf angle
spanning horizontally between concrete columns.

3. Stiffeners
60 × 60 × 3.2 mm horizontal steel square
hollow section welded to steel angle as
stiffener. Vertical 60 × 60 × 3.2 mm steel
square hollow sections at 1120 mm centres as
secondary supports to angle.

4. Glazing bar
30 × 20 × 1.5 mm steel square hollow section
welded to steel angle in 300 mm lengths with
20 mm gaps between to allow ventilation.

5. Upper glazing bead
20 × 37 × 20 × 3 mm polyester powder coated
aluminium glazing angle bolted to steel shelf
angle.

6. Lower glazing bead
130 × 27 × 3 mm polyester powder coated
aluminium glazing angle bolted to steel shelf
angle.

7. Glazing
8 mm thick toughened cast glass with ripple
pattern. Height varies from 876 mm at bottom of
façades to 1852 mm at top.

8. Sealant
Continuous silicon seal with backing support.

9. Spacers
6 mm thick rubber spacer pads 300 mm long
with 20 mm gaps between to allow ventilation.

10. Inner skin
16 mm thick three-layer polycarbonate inner
skin held on 4 sides in aluminium channel fixed
to steel frame.

11. Primary structure
350 × 350 mm reinforced concrete column.

12. Corner steelwork
200 × 90 × 9 × 14 mm continuous unequal
steel angle bracket bolted to concrete column
via 140 long × 6 mm thick steel cleats.
200 × 90 × 9 × 14 mm unequal steel angle
vertical corner trim welded to angle bracket.

13. External translucent wall
See section through glazing support shelf for
construction.

14. External wall – rainscreen cladding
80 × 24 mm dark stained cedar boards
screwed to battens.
60 × 36 mm preservative treated softwood
battens at 900 mm centres approx.
Building paper breather membrane.
12 mm sheathing plywood.
150 × 50 mm E-profile galvanised steel
studs.
100 mm foil-backed rigid insulation.
Two-layers 12.5 mm plasterboard dry lining with
aluminium angle shadow-gap edge trims where
dry lining meets polycarbonate.

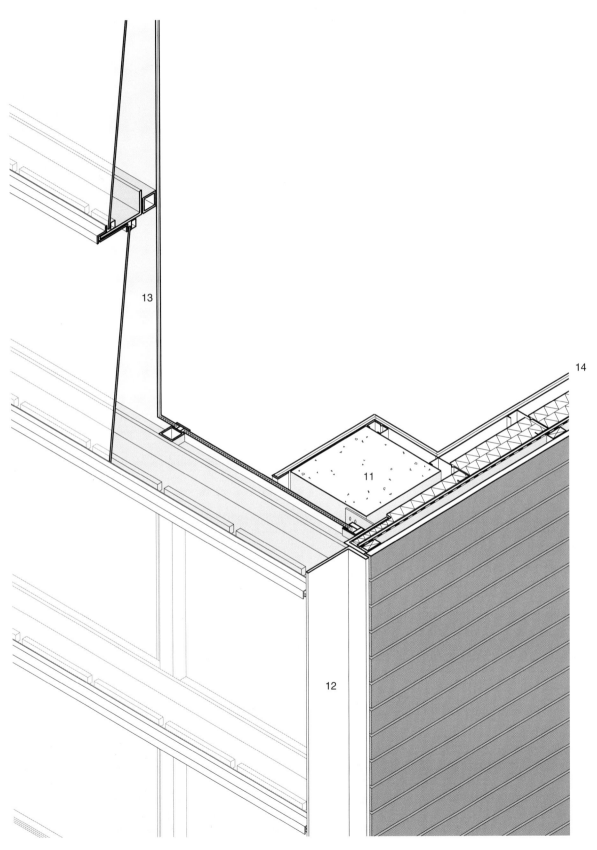

Cut-away section through corner

The Public Gallery, West Bromwich

Architect: Alsop Architects
Building Envelope Subcontractor: Richardson Roofing Ltd

The Public has been described as Europe's largest community arts development, incorporating gallery and events spaces, workspaces, a bar and restaurant in a huge box enclosure.

A self-supporting envelope encloses a single massive volume. Inside, a splayed tapering steel H-frame supports the roof, a mid-level 'table' floor and all the independent forms which populate the space. 'Jelly Bean' windows appear to have been cut out of the cladding in dotted lines along the façades.

The 700 mm thick envelope comprises three layers – an outer rainscreen, a weather-tight skin and an inner lining – all supported off a steel frame which is restrained by the main steelwork. The weather-tight layer is formed from proprietary composite insulated cladding panels supported outside the steel frame on steel cladding rails. The inner lining is perforated sinusoidal cladding, painted pink and fixed to steel trays which are fixed to the steel frame on steel cleats. Mineral fibre in the trays provides thermal insulation and acoustic attenuation for the main space. A layer of black geotextile prevents the insulation being visible through the perforations. The rainscreen is sinusoidal aluminium cladding fixed to vertically aligned aluminium decking riveted to the composite cladding panels. The outer skin is painted with a duo-tone system which has a top coat of mica flakes borne in clear lacquer making the colour appear to change from different angles.

The window openings in the weather-tight layer are rectangular. Aluminium framed curtain wall glazing sits in the plane of the composite panels with its edges covered by steel flashings with compressible seals. Putting the glazing in the central layer meant the jelly-bean windows could be cut out of the rainscreen and inner lining without the complication of vapour and weather-proofing. A pink powder coated curved aluminium trim frames the opening in the rainscreen. Internally, kerfed MDF is curved around the opening and

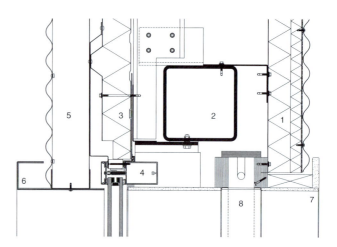

Detail section through window head, scale 1:10

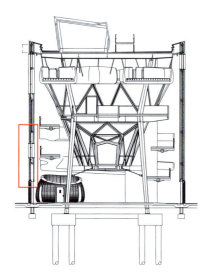

Section with area of detail shown in red, scale 1:500

fixed to the steel tray. A continuous plywood trough contains a cold cathode lighting tube and stiffens the MDF lining.

If a pane of glass needs replacing, however, the external flashing and cladding must be removed to get at the curtain wall glazing frame – an event that has already occurred, raising heated comments in the local press.

1. Inner lining
0.7 mm perforated steel sinusoidal cladding, colour pink, fixed with self-tapping screws. Black geotextile membrane to hide insulation behind.
30 mm semi-rigid mineral fibre thermal insulation.
60 mm mineral fibre quilt acoustic insulation.
90 mm thick steel tac tray spanning vertically between steels.

2. Self-supporting façade structure
254 × 254 × 107 mm vertical steel universal columns (UC) at 8800 mm centres.
200 × 200 × 8 mm horizontal steel square hollow section (SHS) beams at 4200 mm centres.

3. Weather-tight layer
140 × 90 mm cold rolled steel C-section cladding rails.
80 mm thick composite insulated cladding panels fixed to cladding rails.
Powder coated 0.7 mm gauge steel flashing externally at all junctions with curtain walling with compressible seal joints.
Vapour barrier continuity strip compressed behind panel internally at all junctions with curtain walling.

4. Window curtain walling
100 × 60 mm proprietary aluminium transom and mullion sections.
Double-glazed sealed unit with 10 mm toughened outer 50/25 HP Brilliant, 22 mm cavity, 8.8 mm laminated clear float inner.
Pressure plates and caps at perimeter where hidden.
Flush silicone joints between panes elsewhere.

5. Rainscreen
100 mm thick 0.9 mm gauge profiled aluminium decking fixed to upstands of composite panels.
0.9 mm gauge sinusoidal aluminium cladding fixed to decking with aluminium rivets.
Cladding and rivets finished with three-layer duo-tone paint system.

6. External window lining
240 mm deep × 75 mm wide 2 mm gauge curved aluminium trim fixed to aluminium decking with self-tapping screws.
10 mm air gap between trim and glass to allow water to drain.

7. Internal window lining
520 mm deep curved 8 mm MDF lining fixed to tac tray.
88 mm × 18 mm MDF edge trim.

8. Window light
80 mm deep × 70 mm wide continuous MDF trough fixed to tac tray.
Cold cathode tube.
Curved pink perspex light cover.

9. Ground floor curtain walling
175 × 50 mm proprietary aluminium mullion sections.
Double-glazed sealed unit with 10 mm toughened clear float outer, 16 mm cavity, 8.8 mm laminated Ruby Red inner.
Pressure plates and caps at perimeter where hidden.
Flush silicone joints between panes elsewhere.

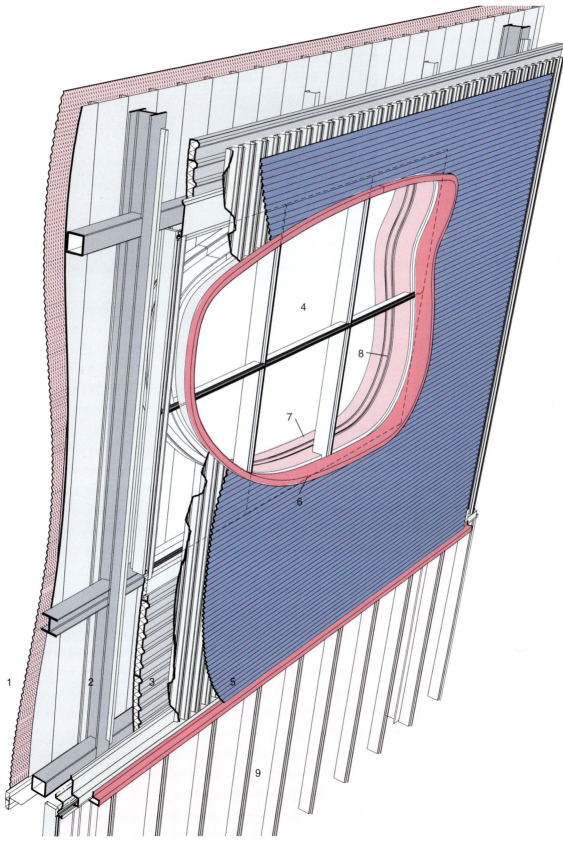

Cut-away section through typical window in external envelope

Photo credit: de Rijke Marsh Morgan

Photo credit: Alex de Rijke

Kingsdale School Auditorium Dulwich, London

Architect: de Rijke Marsh Morgan Architects
Structural Engineer: Michael Hadi Associates
Subcontractor: Timber Engineering Connections

The renovation of Kingsdale School, originally designed in 1959 by Leslie Martin, was set up as a demonstration project funded by the Department for Education and Skills as part of the Architecture Foundation's School Works initiative. The first phase makes a spectacular improvement to the school environment by throwing a translucent roof over its existing 3200 m^2 courtyard.

The three-layer ETFE (Ethylene TetrafluoroEthylene) roof membrane is supported on a line of lightweight steel trusses that rest on the existing walls of the building. There was no need for additional supports because the engineers calculated that the wind load on the courtyard elevations would be reduced by 30–40%. Two of the three layers of the ETFE membrane are screen printed with a pattern that reduces natural daylight and overheating.

The centrepiece of the courtyard is a 314-seat auditorium and library. A geodesic timber structure encloses a space for assemblies, screenings, lectures, performances and music events.

The auditorium seating has the same bent birch-faced plywood profile as the school's standard 1960s classroom chair and is manufactured by the same company. The seats are fixed with steel angles to pre-cast concrete planks supported on steel beams to form a rake. Steel columns carry the loads down to concrete pad foundations.

Photo credit: Alex de Rijke

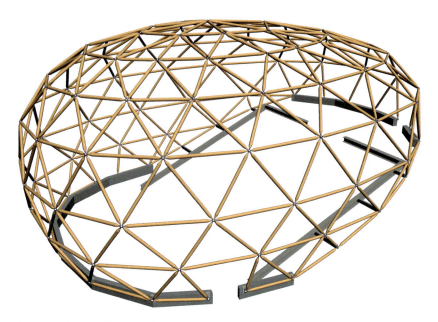

Isometric showing timber auditorium structure

Site plan with auditorium shown in red, scale 1:4000

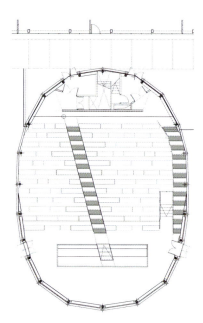

Auditorium plan, scale 1:400

Entrance   Auditorium

Section through auditorium with area of detail shown in red, scale 1:2000

The irregularly shaped geodesic enclosure is supported off the first floor walkway at the back, the edge of the concrete steps around the sides and by concrete plinth stones at the front. At a typical node, spherical metal connectors bring together six 150 mm diameter larch poles. Most connectors are aluminium for lightness but those at the base are steel so they can be welded to plates and bolted to steelwork or a concrete plinth. The larch poles have a threaded bar resin bonded into each end. The bars are screwed into pre-drilled holes in the connectors, each one different due to the irregular shape of the dome. 15 mm birch-faced plywood panels were factory cut and fixed with lost-head nails internally and externally. Mineral fibre quilt insulation 150 mm thick is sandwiched in between with a layer of plasterboard fixed to the back of the outer plywood face for acoustic insulation. A disc of acoustic membrane, made from rubber with a mineral additive, is fixed to both sides of each node point to reduce sound transfer.

Birch plywood sound reflectors hang over the stage and a pattern of Melatech foam triangles has been bonded to the plywood walls as sound absorbent.

1. Exterior cladding
15 mm birch-faced plywood triangles, factory cut with 20 mm radius corners fixed to noggins with lost-head nails.
15 mm gaps between adjacent boards for tolerance.
Class 1 intumescent clear sealant finish.

2. Timber structure
150 mm diameter larch poles with tapered ends. Threaded bar resin bonded into end of pole, diameter varies 16–20 mm.
140 mm diameter metal connector with holes pre-drilled and tapped to receive threaded bars. Connector and bars aluminium generally, steel at base connections and in high tensile load areas.

3. Secondary timberwork
147 × 35 mm softwood noggins nailed to poles.

72 × 35 mm softwood battens behind plywood joints.

4. Acoustic insulation
12.5 mm plasterboard fixed to rear of external plywood.
150 mm mineral wool quilt compressed to 134 mm.
750 mm diameter 2.5 mm thick acoustic membrane discs fixed to both sides of poles around all connectors.
Mineral wool quilt packed behind membrane around steel node connector.

5. Internal cladding
Black DPM (damp-proof membrane) vapour barrier to give consistent shadow line behind plywood.
15 mm birch-faced plywood triangles, factory cut with 20 mm radius corners fixed to noggins with lost-head nails.

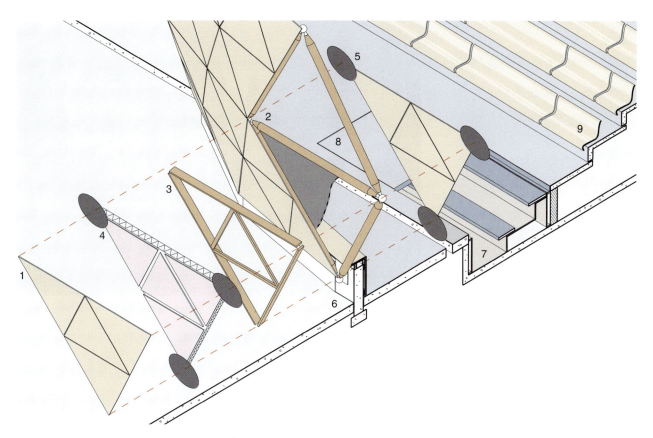

Exploded section through auditorium wall and floor

15 mm gaps between adjacent boards for tolerance.
Class 1 intumescent clear sealant finish.

6. Ground level support
485 × 250 × 725 mm high in-situ concrete plinths.
Steel node connector welded to steel circular hollow section bracket welded to steel plate, all bolted to concrete plinth.
Fluorescent batten light fittings screwed to poles concealed beneath skirt.

7. Pit with recessed seating
Demountable seating box made from 18 mm WBP plywood fins clad in 18 mm

WBP plywood panels all faces screw and glued.
Carpet to riser, going and back of seat.
Brushed stainless steel angle frame projecting 3 mm proud of concrete to form resin stop.

8. Removable covers to pit
18 mm plywood on softwood carcass.
Resin floor finish.

9. Auditorium seating
1005 × 320 mm × 90 mm thick pre-cast concrete planks spanning between steel beams below.
Curved 18 mm birch-faced plywood seat bolted to continuous steel angle brackets.

Moggerhanger House, Bedfordshire

Restoration Architects: Inskip + Jenkins Architects
Original Architect: John Soane (1790–1816)

John Soane began work at Moggerhanger House in 1790 and continued to modify it in several phases over a period of 25 years. The house was sold in 1857 and after passing through various hands was bought by the county council and used as a hospital, during which time it suffered significant alteration. Restoration work has revealed a two-storey 'tribune', a name Soane coined from a Roman term for a kind of open hallway. Tribunes were incorporated in various Soane country house interiors but they were all filled in during the nineteenth century as unappreciative owners sought more floor space.

At Moggerhanger a roof lantern and an opening in the first floor have been reinstated to bring light down into a lobby deep in the plan between the main stair and the rooms on the east side of the house. An intricate spatial relationship between the main staircase, the adjacent lobby and the dressing room above has been re-established.

The roof of the lantern is supported on thin brass glazing bars which are tied together by a brass ring at the head. A lead roof is supported on timber boards spanning across an oak ring-beam which sits on the brass ring. The glass is laminated with an outer layer of centrifugally spun cylinder glass and an inner layer of modern toughened glass for safety. Used in all windows and roof lights, the cylinder glass is made by an eighteenth century process and has a distinctive rippled texture.

In various situations a surface effect was used to make a cheap material resemble a more expensive one. The first floor opening, for example, has a delicate wrought-iron balustrade with a green finish to make it look like bronze. Stain has been applied to the softwood floorboards to give the appearance of hardwood and 'graining' has been applied to woodwork in the hall and dining room to make it resemble a more expensive timber.

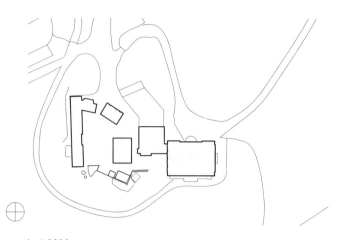

Site plan, scale 1:2000

Colour was used to differentiate between wall planes and edges. Grey painted beads, mouldings and linings to openings appear to carry the weight of the building. Wall planes are painted an earthy pink, separated from the grey corners by incised mouldings. The main walls are 'flatted', a technique where the top gloss paint coat is stippled with a brush while still tacky to make a textured surface. By adhering strictly to eighteenth century construction methods, Inskip & Jenkins are trying to leave Moggerhanger as close as possible to the state Soane intended.

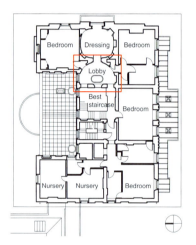

First floor plan with area of detail shown in red, scale 1:500

1. Roof lantern
Softwood framing to opening in roof.
Oak ring-beam frame to form lantern roof.
50 × 12 mm unpolished brass glazing bars with brass beads profiled to match timber window beads.
Laminated glass made up from 3 mm cylinder glass resin bonded to 4 mm toughened inner pane.
Lead sheet roof finish secured with clips.
25 mm loose-tongued softwood boards upper layer.
25 mm loose-tongued joinery quality softwood board soffit painted off-white.
Original moulded plaster rose fixed to soffit on stainless steel wires.

2. First floor ceiling
6 mm timber lath.
25 mm plaster.
Ceilings and cornices painted off-white.

3. First floor
25 mm softwood Deal floorboards stained dark reddish brown.
Softwood joists.
Straw and lime pugging on softwood board fixed to joists with softwood battens.
6 mm timber lath.
25 mm plaster painted white.

Single line of softwood balls as cornice painted off-white.

4. First floor opening
Softwood framing to floor opening.
Softwood corner beads painted white.
Vertical floor edge plastered and painted off-white.

5. Balustrade
Wrought-iron balustrade with bronzed green finish.
Mahogany handrail.

6. Internal wall
Solid brick load-bearing walls.
25 mm three-coat lime plaster.
Pink 'flatted' paint finish.
Softwood corner beads and mouldings painted grey.
Linings to reveals painted grey.

7. Blind opening
Existing opening infilled with brickwork.
50 × 25 mm vertical softwood battens.
6 mm softwood lath.
25 mm three-coat lime plaster.

8. Ground floor
25 mm softwood Deal floorboards stained dark reddish brown.
Softwood joists on brick sleeper walls.

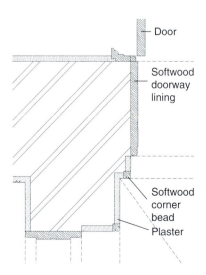

Detail plan of typical door jamb and mouldings, scale 1:20

— Door

— Softwood doorway lining

— Softwood corner bead
— Plaster

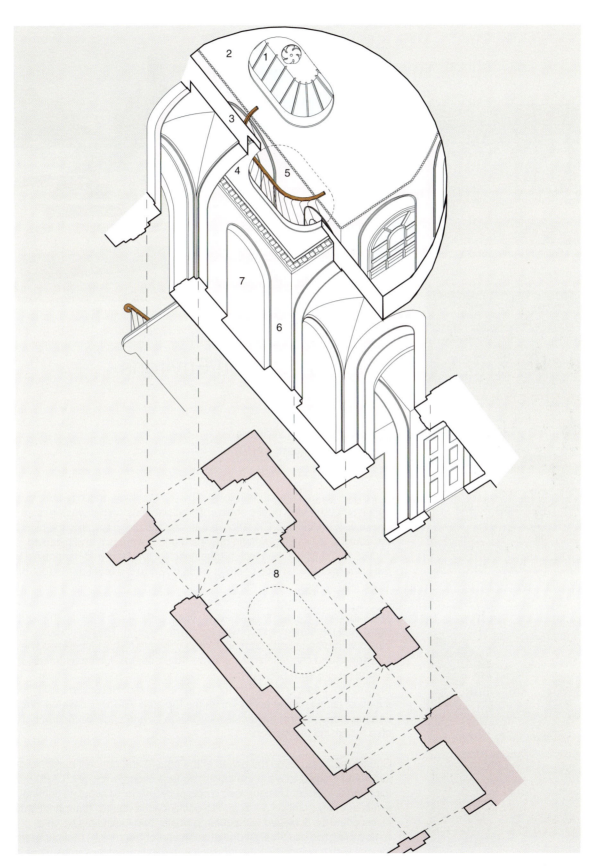

Cut-away section through tribune looking up towards lantern with ground floor plan projected below

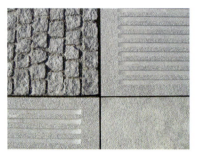

Photo credit: Morley von Sternberg

Photo credit: Morley von Sternberg

Photo credit: Morley von Sternberg

Tower of London Environs, London

Architect: Stanton Williams
Lighting Consultant: LAPD

Tower Hill, the main approach to the Tower of London, has been transformed by a new 200 m long public square. Three pavilions on the western side house visitor facilities. The whole square ramps down towards the river to the south at a 1 in 20 gradient, providing equal ambulant and disabled access to the whole area without the need for landings and handrails. On the eastern side a terrace of steps leads down to the moat at the foot of the Tower wall.

The steps act as a ha-ha. There is no balustrade at the edge so the square has a very direct relationship with the tower beyond. The main square is paved with granite setts on a reinforced concrete slab which allows fine tolerances and can take emergency vehicle loadings. Flame textured Lanhelin granite paving from Brittany has been laid in bands across the square, along the western edge, and is used for the terrace steps. Recessed LED lights and a strip of tactile paving behind mark the top step. Grooves have been routed into the stone to form the tactile recognition paving and into the front of each step for nosing recognition.

Granite benches define the edges of the square and conceal metal halide luminaires angled to wash the paving surface evenly with light. LAPD (Lighting & Product Design) used a computer model to simulate lighting levels at every point on a 1 m grid to convince the council that park lighting levels could be achieved without lamp posts. Two luminaires sit on a removable stainless steel sledge at each end of the bench. Stainless steel louvres with a polycarbonate diffuser located in front of the lamps hinge open for maintenance. The lamps can be unplugged and removed by folding down the top boom of the sledge.

Photo credit: Morley von Sternberg

Site section, scale 1:4000

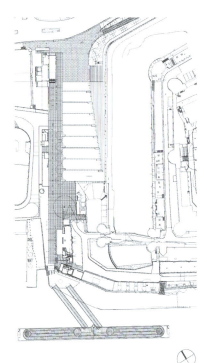

Site plan, scale 1:3000

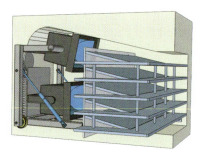

Model of stone recess showing
louvres and lighting sledge

1. Typical step
1494 × 730 × 160 mm flame textured Lanhelin
granite step laid to 1:70 fall.
20 mm horizontal shadow gap to next step.
6 mm joints between adjacent stones pointed
with semi-dry 1:3 lime:sand mortar.
Two 5 × 5 mm nosing recognition grooves
routed out of step, continuous between stones
and stopping 100 mm short of end of step.
Minimum 40 mm semi-dry 1:3 cement:sand
mortar bed.
Minimum 200 mm thick reinforced concrete
sub-base.

2. Top step
1494 × 694 × 160 mm flame textured Lanhelin
granite step laid to 1:70 fall.
28 mm diameter hole drilled in centre of each
stone with 48 × 11 mm deep diameter recess
at top for flush mounted LED light fitting to
indicate top of steps.

3. Tactile recognition
1494 × 694 × 75 mm flame textured Lanhelin
granite step with tactile recognition corduroy
pattern formed from twelve 25 × 5 mm grooves
routed into granite, continuous between stones
but stopping 100 mm short of end of step.
6 mm joints between adjacent stones pointed
with semi-dry 1:3 lime:sand mortar.
50 mm semi-dry 1:3 cement:sand mortar bed.
Reinforced concrete sub-base.

4. Paving to main square
90 × 90 × 75 mm thick granite setts with
cropped faces laid in stretcher bond on 1:20
slope.
135 × 90 × 75 mm sett at beginning of
alternate rows to avoid cuts.
10 mm joints between adjacent setts pointed
with 1: ¼:3 cement:lime:sand.
50 mm dry 1:3 cement:sand mortar bed.
Reinforced concrete sub-base.

5. Granite paving band
1293 × 490 × 75 mm flame textured Lanhelin
granite slabs.
50 mm semi-dry 1:3 cement:sand mortar bed.

Reinforced concrete sub-base.

6. Drainage
130 mm wide polymer-concrete channel drains
at 18 m centres down slope with stainless steel
grating.
125 mm high × 10 mm thick stainless steel
plate restraining stone on slope with six 100 ×
75 × 10 mm thick stainless steel slotted fixing
plates welded at 450 mm centres fixed on shims
to concrete sub-base with M8 stainless steel
expansion anchors.

7. Bench plinth
2550 × 410 × 380 mm high reinforced concrete
plinth.
Solid Lanhelin granite flame textured side
pieces.

8. Bench top
4000 × 990 × 150 mm thick Lanhelin granite
seat in three pieces with flame textured top
and sides on concealed stainless steel
brackets bolted to concrete plinth through
levelling shims.

9. Louvres
8 mm thick stainless steel louvre assembly
with 12° blade upstand spaced apart by 8 mm
diameter rods welded on underside only.
4 mm thick opal polycarbonate sheet diffuser
fixed to louvre assembly with cotter pins.
Louvres swing out on purpose-made hinges
secured via lockable stainless steel security
screw.

10. Lighting sledge
Sledge made up from welded stainless steel
box sections on four wheels.
Two 70-Watt metal halide luminaires angled
differently to wash paving with light.
Two stainless steel gas struts allow assembly to
fold for removal from bench recess.
Luminaires connected with curly cable to IP65
rated socket to allow removal from bench
recess.

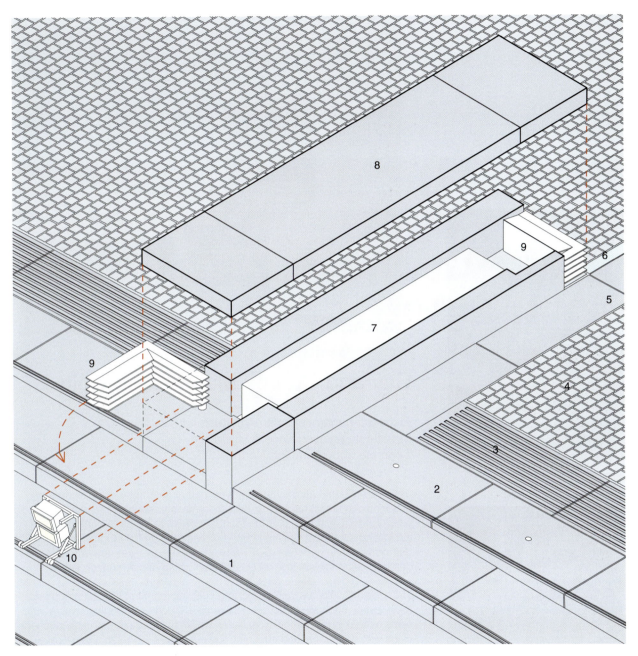

Exploded view of bench and landscaping

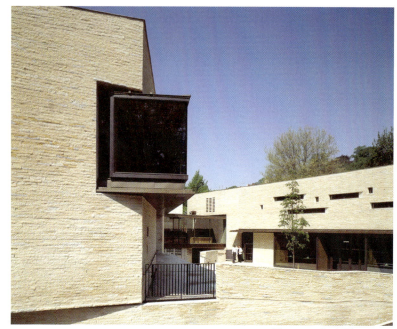

City and County Museum, Lincoln

Architect: Panter Hudspith Architects
Structural Engineer: Price & Myers
Concrete Subcontractor: Northfield Construction

Set on a hill dominated by the city's cathedral, the museum is deliberately anti-iconic. It is located on a scheduled ancient monument so excavation was kept to a minimum and the foundations reuse some existing piles of a demolished car park to limit disturbance to the archaeological remains. Self-compacting concrete (SCC) was used extensively to deal with complex geometries and to achieve an exceptionally high quality surface finish.

The external walls are self-supporting split-faced limestone restrained back to an in-situ concrete structure. The roofs are generally sloping concrete flat slabs except in the exhibition galleries where they are more steeply pitched slabs with a diagonal fold changing the pitch from 22° to 28°. To achieve the precise angles required in the gallery roof slabs an initial level deck was built on a scaffold and a series of progressively higher softwood formers was built off it to support the actual formwork deck.

SCC was used to form each 42 m long slab in just three pours. A top shutter was required, demanding complex custom-made formwork. The natural colour of SCC is light so no additional pigment was added. Three such roofs form a saw-tooth roof light array, bringing north light deep into the galleries.

In public areas the concrete walls are left exposed. Planed timber boards of varying thickness from 18 to 21 mm were fixed to the inner face of a proprietary shutter system to intensify the board markings in the concrete. SCC picks up an incredibly fine level of timber grain detail and retains very sharp arrises. Some areas internally are clad in oak boarding the same 75 mm width as the formwork boards and the external limestone cladding so the building's primary materials all have a similar scale grain.

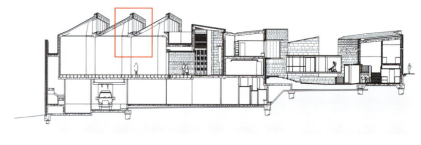

North-south section with area of detail shown in red, scale 1:600

Site and roof plan, scale 1:3000

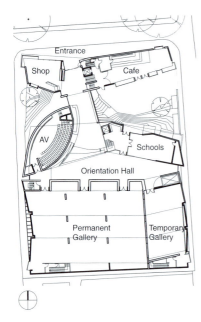

Upper floor plan, scale 1:1000

1. External wall
200 mm thick self-compacting concrete structural wall.
Outer face covered with insulation, cavity and split-faced limestone.
Inner face board-marked left exposed.
40 × 15 mm shadow gap cast in between wall and roof.

2. External wall formwork
Proprietary shuttering system in varying width modules with 21 mm plywood face sprayed with release agent.
Additional waling (beams clamped to both sides of formwork and bolted through) over lower half of wall height to resist hydrostatic pressure of self-compacting concrete.
Additional 21 mm plywood layer over lower half of wall height to resist hydrostatic pressure of self-compacting concrete.

3. Internal wall formwork
Proprietary shuttering system in varying width modules with 21 mm plywood face.
75 mm wide tongued and grooved smooth planed redwood boards nailed to plywood face. Thickness of boards varies from 18 to 21 mm to give relief to concrete.
Wax applied to face of boards followed by mist coat of release agent.
40 × 15 mm chamfered batten to form shadow gap between wall and roof.

4. Concrete kicker beam
1700 mm wide × 600 mm deep self-compacting concrete kicker beam spanning between concrete columns at nominal 12 m centres.

Roof light aluminium curtain walling sits on beam.

5. Roof
300 mm thick self-compacting concrete slab (pitch cranks from 22° to 28°).
Outer face to be finished with terne coated stainless steel standing seam roofing on 18 mm WBP plywood on mineral wool insulation on vapour barrier.
Concrete soffit to be left exposed.

6. Internal roof formwork
Shutter supported off floor below on proprietary metal frames and jacks.
Gallery floor propped from below in basement temporarily to resist load of concrete and formwork.
Shuttering formed from proprietary metal beams with 21 mm plywood face.
Wax applied to upper face of plywood followed by mist coat of release agent.

7. External roof formwork
Custom-made shutter formed from 150 × 50 mm softwood joists with 21 mm plywood face to suit cranked form of roof.
Galvanised steel waling beams bolted across shutter to spread weight of concrete.
Wax applied to lower face of plywood followed by mist coat of release agent.

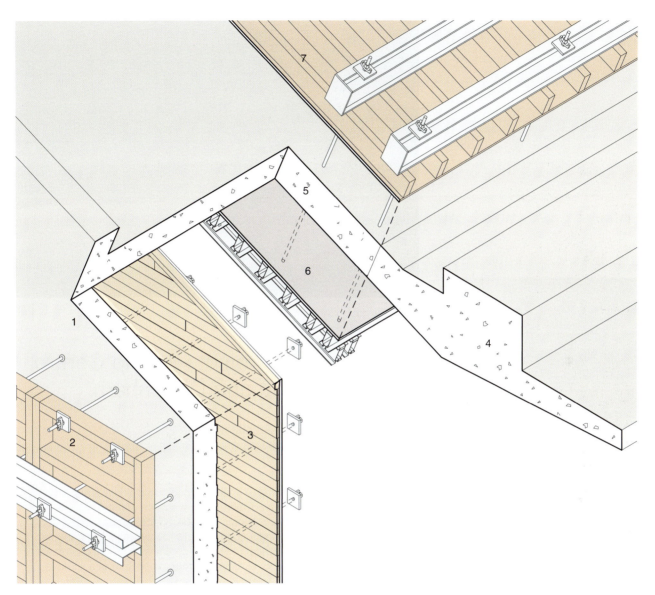

Section through gallery wall and roof showing formwork and concrete only

A13 Artscape Project – Pump Control House, Barking and Dagenham

Building Design: de Paor Architects
Lighting Design: Clare Brew

The A13 Artscape project aims to improve conditions for residents, workers, pedestrians and drivers along a 6 km stretch of the A13 trunk road in east London. Various artworks have been incorporated into road improvement works including two pedestrian subways, two roundabouts and an underpass. The pump control house contains electrical equipment to operate pumps which remove rainwater from the bottom of a six-lane underpass.

Eight 160 mm thick pre-cast concrete panels are supported off a steel frame of 150 × 150 × 10 mm angle posts with 200 × 90 mm channel horizontal members. From the outside the panels interlock and appear to form a solid mass floating slightly above the grass. The roof is profiled galvanised steel decking on purlins with two aluminium framed roof lights all hidden below the tops of the slabs. The concrete is made from white cement with Portland stone aggregate. The surface has been acid etched, polished and then sealed with an anti-graffiti coating. The access doors are 85 mm thick pre-cast concrete panels cast into a 150 × 75 × 10 mm steel angle frame. Three 280 mm high, concealed hinges are bolted to the doors and to the steel frame. All internal steelwork is painted bright orange.

Cast into the concrete are 456 solid 40 mm diameter acrylic rods. Millions of different colours can be created by nine red, green and blue LEDs mounted in a case which fits over the back of each rod. A computer in the control house can be remotely programmed with changing sequences. Light seems to glow from within the concrete as if the building is pumping with colour.

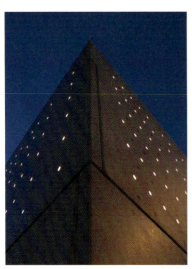

Photo credit: Graham Bizley

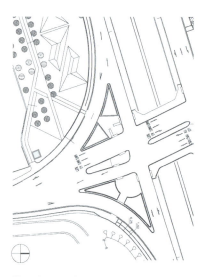

Site plan, scale 1:2000

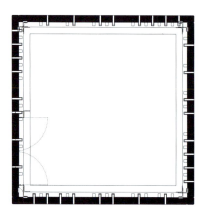

Floor plan, scale 1:100

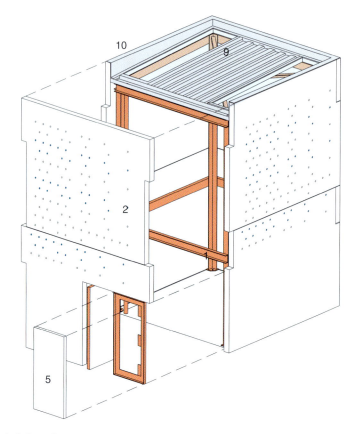

Exploded view of pump control house

1. Steel frame
150 × 150 × 10mm angle posts in corners.
200 × 90mm horizontal parallel flange channel.
Steel painted with zinc-rich epoxy shop primer, micaceous iron oxide shop intermediate coat and two top coats on site.

2. Precast Concrete Panels
Eight 160mm precast concrete panels hung off steel frame on mild steel brackets.
10mm gap between top and bottom panels filled with recessed double mastic seal.
Top and bottom panels located together by threaded stainless steel dowels set in grout.
Panels made from C40 concrete with white cement and Portland stone aggregate.
10 × 10mm chamfers on all external arises.
All exposed faces acid-etched, polished and sealed with anti-graffiti coating.

3. Concrete panel cleats
150mm length bracket made from 200 × 100 × 10mm steel angle bolted to posts.
Vertically slotted holes in long leg and horizontally slotted holes in short leg to allow adjustment on site.
Concrete panels bolted to brackets via cast-in channels on rear.

4. Door over-panel support
2010mm length 80 × 80 × 10mm steel angle bracket welded to 150 × 75 × 10mm steel angle cast into underside of concrete panel over door and bolted to steel frame on shims.

5. Concrete doors
Two inward opening 85mm thick precast concrete doors cast into 2090 × 990mm frames made from 150 × 75 × 10mm steel angles.

6. Door hinges
Three 280mm long 3-flag stainless steel hinges per leaf.
Three 280 × 100 × 10mm steel plates welded to door frame and bolted to hinges.
Three 150 × 135 × 135mm brackets welded up from 10mm flats bolted to steel posts and bolted to hinges.

7. Lighting
210mm long × 40mm diameter acrylic rods cast into concrete panel (115 each side).
Nine 24 volt LEDs (3 red, 3 blue, 3 green) wired back to control panel.
80mm long × 60mm diameter aluminium cap to fit on to end of acrylic rod and enclose LED fittings creating heat sink for LED circuit pad.
Clip-in plug fitting.

8. Electrical supply
50 × 25mm horizontal galvanised steel cable trays at approx. 450mm centres fixed to rear of concrete panels.

9. Roof
0.9mm guage galvanised steel profiled sheet roof on four 122mm deep Z-section purlins.
Two 3500 × 950mm proprietary aluminium framed glazed rooflights.

10. Flashings
Pressed metal flashings shot-fired to concrete.
Flashing stops 10mm short of front face of panels and falls to inside.

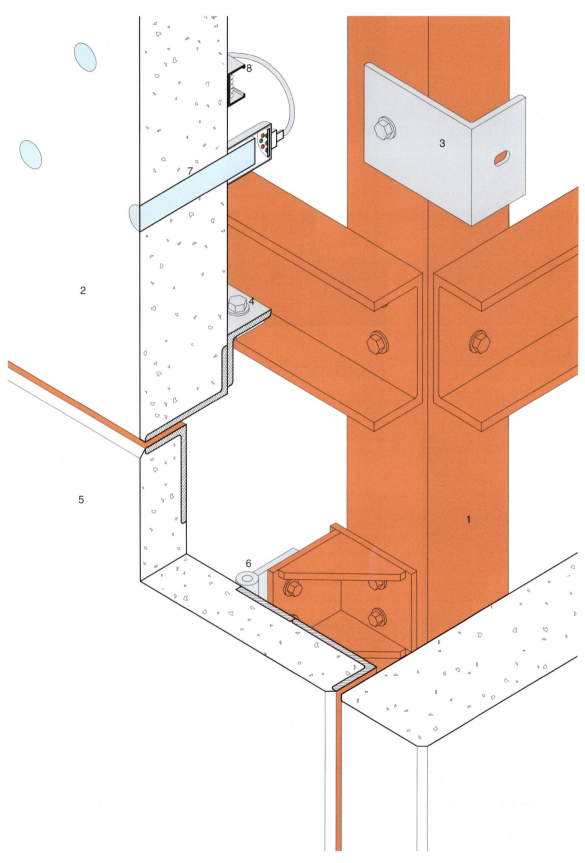

Cut-away section through corner

Metropolitan Cathedral Campus, Liverpool

Architect: Falconer Chester Hall Architects
Landscape Architect: Landscape Projects

A new public space and a flight of ceremonial steps have been created on the south side of Liverpool's Metropolitan Cathedral making a spectacular new approach to the entrance and addressing the Anglican Cathedral at the other end of Hope Street. The public space will be flanked on one side by new offices for high-tech businesses and by a visitor centre for the cathedral on the other. An alternative route avoiding the steps climbs 8 m up a 1:20 ramp paved with resin bonded gravel as it sweeps across the landscaped roof of the visitor centre.

The concrete rear wall of the visitor centre retains the earth behind, buttressed by a steel roof structure. Huge 2 m cubes of polystyrene have been used to build up the landscape slopes whilst minimising imposed loads on the roof. The rough shapes are covered in soil and planted with *Lonicera* (honeysuckle).

The entrance façade to the steps is glazed. The other exposed wall follows the curve of the street and is clad in 120 mm thick Welsh slate. The wall leans back at an angle of 4° and gradually disappears underground as the road rises up next to it. The slate is self-supporting with stainless steel ties back to a concrete blockwork inner leaf. Above the 17 m long strip window the slate is supported on a stainless steel shelf angle fixed back to the roof steelwork on 450 mm deep brackets at 500 mm centres. The shelf angle is facetted in 1400 mm lengths so that the slate could be laid to a curve. The balustrade on top is made from stainless steel mesh clamped into a stainless steel frame supported by paired stainless steel flat uprights. The slow curving façade, with its restrained palette of slate and stainless steel, echoes the scale and grace of the Cathedral.

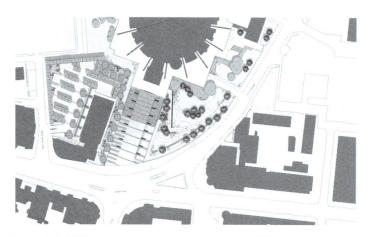

Site plan, scale 1:3000

Plan with area of detail shown in red, scale 1:1500

1. Primary structure
203 × 203 UC (universal column) columns bolted to 1500 × 1500 mm concrete pad bases. Intumescent paint finish to exposed steel.

2. Ground floor
75 mm reinforced screed.
Isolating polythene layer.
30 mm rigid urethane insulation.
175 mm thick ground-bearing reinforced concrete slab thickening to 450 mm at edges.
Bituminous sheet tanking membrane on 100 mm sand blinding.

3. Retaining wall
12.5 mm plasterboard inner lining.
25 mm cavity and 50 mm rigid urethane insulation between 75 × 50 mm softwood battens.
300 mm thick reinforced concrete wall.
Bituminous sheet tanking membrane with drainage coil at foot of wall.
Eggcrate type drainage sheet.

4. Roof Structure
150 mm thick reinforced concrete slab on profiled galvanised steel deck.
457 × 165 mm primary UBs (universal beams) at nominal 5000 mm centres running front to back and buttressing retaining wall.
254 × 146 mm secondary UBs at nominal 3000 mm centres between primary beams.

5. Lower retaining wall
300 mm thick in-situ concrete wall with two coats mineral paint finish.
400 mm wide holes in wall adjacent to drainage outlets from soft landscape area.

6. Soft Landscaping
300 mm thick *Lonicera* ground cover planting.
400 mm min. top soil on 150 mm sub-soil.
Expanded polystyrene block fill.
Geotextile membrane.
Eggcrate type drainage sheet.
125 mm extruded polystyrene insulation.
Bituminous sheet tanking membrane.
Screed laid to 1:80 fall.

7. Hard Landscaping
600 × 400 × 50 mm concrete pavers on PVC spacers with 100 mm sedum strips between rows.

50 mm gravel drainage strips at edges.
Geotextile on eggcrate drainage sheet.
125 mm extruded polystyrene insulation.
Bituminous sheet tanking membrane.
Screed laid to 1:80 fall.

8. External Wall
140 mm thick 7 N/mm^2 blockwork inner leaf.
100 mm cavity with 35 mm partial fill insulation.
2 layers 140 mm thick 20 N/mm^2 blockwork.
120 mm thick coursed Bethesda slate outer leaf made up from 400–800 mm long × 100–200 mm high blocks. Front face pillared, top and bottom face riven finish, sawn at either end.

9. Window
50 mm aluminium curtain walling box section frame fixed to channel at head and angle at cill. Double glazed sealed units.
Polyester powder coated pressed aluminium cill.
Rendered soffit board bonded to underside of stone support angle.
Stainless steel shelf angle to support slate fixed to roof steelwork on 450 mm deep stainless steel brackets at 500 mm centres.

10. Balustrade
Uprights bolted down to concrete slab at 2020 mm centres formed from paired 100 × 10 mm stainless steel flats with continuously welded 20 × 10 mm spacer.
200 × 40 mm channel handrail formed from folded 6 mm stainless steel plate bolted to uprights with stainless steel security bolts.
Rigid stainless steel mesh fixed to uprights with 40 × 6 mm stainless steel flat cover strips.
40 × 40 × 6 mm stainless steel angle bolted between uprights to form bottom restraint.
500 × 30 mm flame-textured granite copings doweled to adjacent stones and resin-anchored to blockwork with stainless steel wire ties.

11. Garden Ramp
2400 mm wide resin bonded 'Rose Pink' gravel on 20 mm thick bitmac wearing course.
40 mm thick bitmac base course on 150 mm fill.
Galvanised steel edging angle.

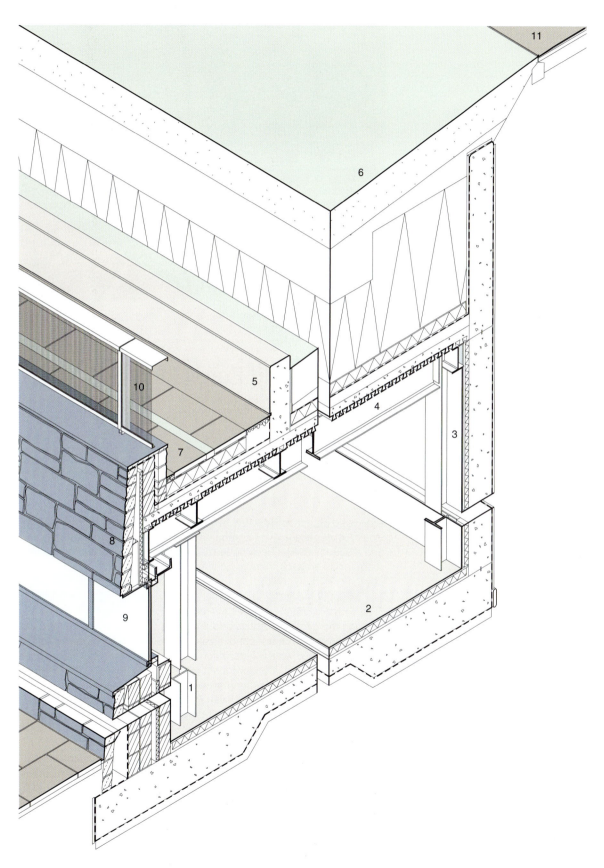

Section through visitor centre roof and external wall

St Paul's Old Ford Church
Bow, London

Architect: Matthew Lloyd Architects
Structural Engineer: Price & Myers
M & E Engineer: Arup

A disused church in Bow has been saved from demolition by the vision of its vicar. An art gallery, gym, community hall, counselling rooms, crèche, café and a sauna have all been squeezed into the existing volume, still leaving room for an area for worship beneath a new timber-clad 'ark'.

The ark sits on eight cranked circular hollow section steel columns partially filled with concrete for stiffness. The front face cantilevers out over the nave carrying the gym floor above and imposing 40 tonne loads into the first row of columns. The ark contains a gallery space, which has a resin floor and painted MDF wall linings which appear to float on light from concealed fluorescent battens. Two layers of fireline board internally and externally provide 1 hour fire protection between the gallery and the nave below. The outside of the ark is clad in 15 mm thick poplar boards, chosen for its blond colour, nailed through the fireline board to a plywood layer behind. The inner and outer skins are supported on a secondary framing system of steel stud channels.

The gallery space is ventilated with air from the nave below, which enters through slots in the timber cladding, drawn up by a mechanical extract in the gallery ceiling. A plenum in the depth of the gallery wall is lined with acoustic foam and contains an acoustic baffle. The grilles are offset to reduce noise transfer between the spaces. Intumescent grilles are fitted to maintain the integrity of the fire barrier.

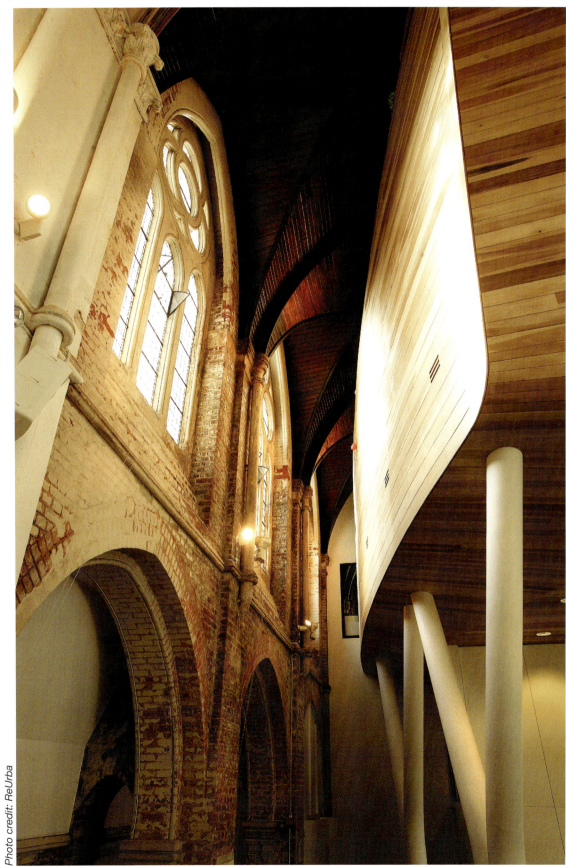

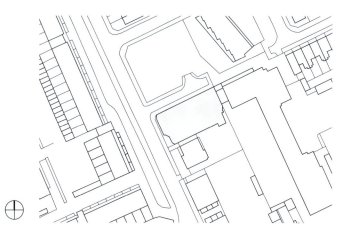

Site plan, scale 1:2000.

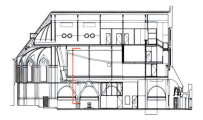

Long section through church with area of detail shown red, scale 1:750.

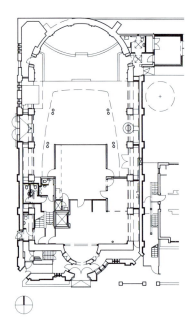

Ground floor plan, scale 1:500.

1. Columns
300 mm diameter CHS (circular hollow section) steel columns cranked to provide bracing.
Concrete pad-base foundations.
Columns filled with concrete to just below knee level.
Intumescent paint to provide 1 hour's fire protection.

2. Steel structure
533 × 210 mm × 122 kg UBs (universal beams) at 4.5 m centres cased in two layers 12.5 mm fireline board for fire protection.
305 × 127 mm × 37 kg UB ties bolted between primary beams.
203 × 203 mm × 46 kg UC (universal column) outrigger beam bolted to UB via steel stub beams to carry outer wall.

3. First floor
140 mm deep concrete slab on trapezoidal galvanised steel decking.
12 mm extruded polystyrene thermal insulation.
98 mm concrete screed with embedded underfloor heating pipes.
2 mm resin floor finish, colour moss green.

4. Ground floor ceiling
150 × 15 mm square-edge poplar boards with 5 mm route to form shadow gap between each board.
Two layers 9 mm plywood.
150 mm steel stud frame.

5. Outer skin
200 × 15 mm square-edge poplar boards with 5 mm route to form shadow gap between each board.
Two layers 12.5 mm fireline board.
Two layers 9 mm plywood.
150 mm mineral fibre quilt insulation.
150 mm steel stud frame.

6. Inner skin
18 mm MDF inner lining to gallery, painted white.
75 × 75 mm softwood battens.
Continuous recessed fluorescent strip lighting at skirting and cornice levels around three sides of gallery.
Two layers 12.5 mm fireline board.
150 mm steel stud frame fixed between 203 × 203 mm × 46 kg UC portal frames at 4.5 m centres.
150 mm mineral fibre quilt insulation.

7. Ceiling
Two layers 12.5 mm fireline board inner lining.
150 mm steel stud frame.
150 mm mineral fibre quilt insulation.
533 × 210 mm × 122 kg UB portal frame at 4.5 m centres.
150 mm mineral fibre quilt insulation.
150 mm steel stud frame
Two layers 12.5 mm fireline board gloss painted white.

8. Ventilation system
Three 150 × 30 mm slots cut in timber boards at nominal 2.4 metre centres.
300 × 150 mm intumescent vent behind slots.
Continuous plenum box with central plasterboard baffle lined with acoustic absorbent foam.
200 × 200 mm intumescent vents with steel grilles at 2.4 m centres offset 800 mm from outer vents to reduce noise transfer.

9. Existing church wall
Existing brickwork walls wire-brushed to remove dirt and left unpainted to dry out.

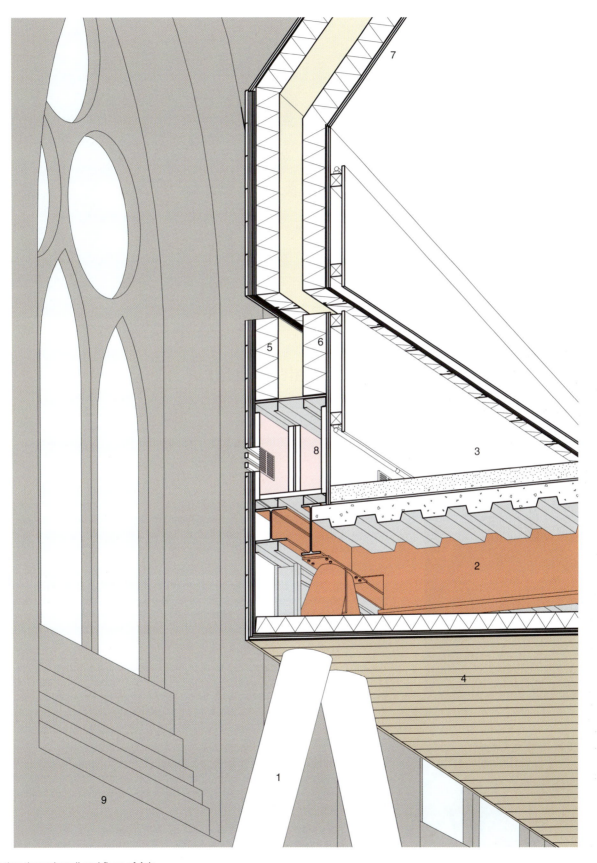

Section through wall and floor of Ark.

Photo credit: David Grandorge

Photo credit: David Grandorge

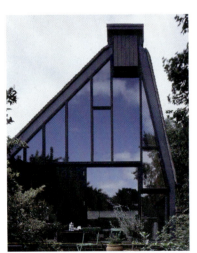

Photo credit: David Grandorge

Photo credit: Morely von Sternberg

Friars Halt Studio
Battle, East Sussex

Architect: Inglis Badrashi Loddo Architects
Structural Engineer: Price & Myers

Drawing inspiration from nearby oast houses, the artist's studio comprises a steeply pitched tiled roof over a partially buried brick plinth containing a garage. The form of the 5 m high timber roof is distorted towards the north side where a full height glazed screen opens the studio to the garden.

The lower floor has uninsulated load-bearing 215 mm brick walls made from handmade Sussex bricks selected from the hottest part of the kiln to give a burnt finish. The studio floor is beam and block with insulation and a floating sand–cement screed. In the studio the brick wall is insulated and lined with WBP (water and boil proof) plywood. A band of frameless clerestory glazing separates the brick wall from the roof above.

The roof structure is supported on four steel posts in the corners bolted to steel spreader beams concealed in the floor, which sit on padstones in the wall. The posts support beams to form portal frames on three sides. The fourth side contains a tie in the form of a steel flat sandwiched between two joists, which follow the timber framing of the glazed screen elevation up and over the doorway.

The roof is designed as three composite planes. Tongued and grooved sarking boards nailed to the rafters provide in-plane stiffness because the normal interaction between battens and rafters is not sufficient to balance the forces created by the asymmetrical form.

Five prefabricated Sapele frames make up the glazed screen with Sapele doors and a top-hinged ventilation panel. Materials internally are left in their natural light coloured state in contrast with the dark stained timber screen and bricks externally.

Photo credit: David Grandorge

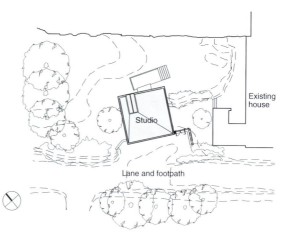

Site plan, scale 1:500

Photo credit: Morely von Sternberg

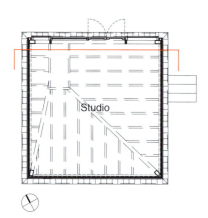

Upper floor plan, scale 1:150

1. Walls
215 mm Sussex handmade Tudor Dark load-bearing brick wall.
215 mm common brickwork below ground level.
Drainage board against outside of wall with liquid applied bituminous DPM inside.
450 × 250 mm mass concrete strip foundations.

2. Ground floor
65 mm sand–cement screed.
Liquid asphaltic tanking membrane.
150 ground-bearing reinforced concrete slab.
Polythene damp-proof membrane.
Sand blinding and hardcore.

3. First floor
65 mm sand–cement screed.
500 gauge polythene damp-proof membrane.
70 mm rigid polyisocyanurate insulation below screed and around perimeter.
Concrete beam and block floor.

4. Steel frame
Four 200 × 100 mm RHS (rectangular hollow section) posts in corners.
200 × 100 mm PFC (parallel flange channel) ring beam on three sides.

5. Tie behind glazed screen
Two 150 × 38 mm softwood horizontal joists sandwiched around 75 × 6 mm mild steel flat.
Two 150 × 38 mm softwood vertical joists sandwiched around 110 × 30 mm mild steel flat to form posts framing doorway and adjacent window.

6. Roof structure
150 × 75 mm softwood rafters at 600 mm centres.
Hips formed from two 150 × 75 mm softwood rafters.
Verge rafters behind glazed screen bolted to 150 × 75 mm steel angle.

7. Roof
200 × 22 mm softwood tongued and grooved sarking boards nailed to rafters.
Polythene vapour barrier.
60 mm rigid polyisocyanurate insulation.
Breather membrane underlay draped into gutter.
25 × 50 mm vertical tannelised softwood battens and 25 × 38 mm horizontal tannelised softwood counter-battens.
Reclaimed handmade clay tiles pegged to battens.

8. Lead box
19 mm WBP plywood lining.
Polythene vapour barrier.
60 mm rigid polyisocyanurate insulation.
Roofing felt underlay.
50 mm continuous ventilation gap.
19 mm WBP plywood on softwood battens.
Code 5 lead sheet finish with batten roll joints on building paper underlay.
Lead apron flashing over tiles below.

9. Glazed screen
170 × 70 mm Sapele primary frame members.
95 × 70 mm Sapele secondary frame members.
Double-glazed 6:12:6 argon filled sealed units with low-E coating fixed with Sapele beads.
57 mm ledged and braced Sapele entrance doors.
57 mm Sapele high level vent panel.

10. Glazed clerestory
Double-glazed 6:12:6 argon filled sealed units with low-E coating butt jointed with silicone sealant.
38 × 25 mm satin anodised aluminium head channel.
93 × 32 mm satin anodised aluminium sill angle.
25 × 25 mm satin anodised aluminium sill angle bead.
Black quarry tile sill over brick wall.

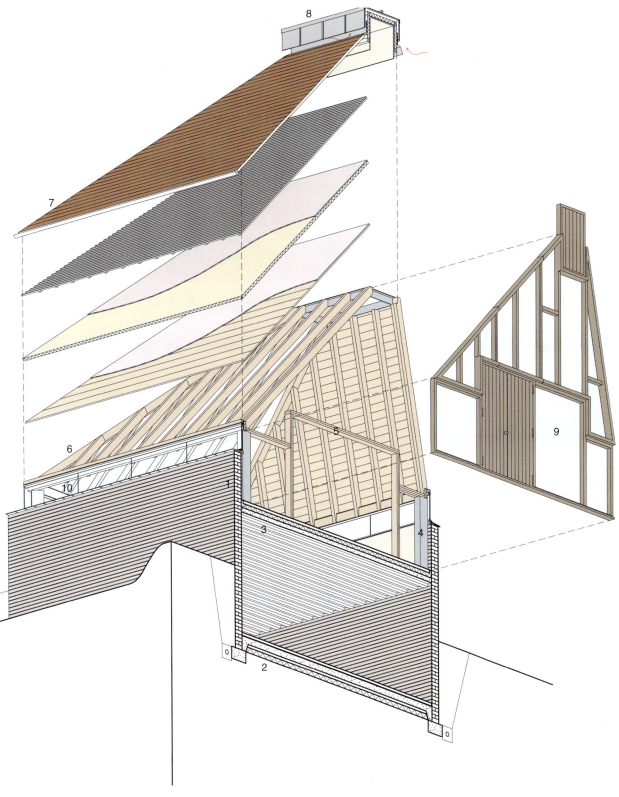

Exploded section

Photo credit: Štěpán Bartoš

Novy Dvur Monastery, Czech Republic

Architect: John Pawson Architects
Associate Architects: Atelier Soukup

Photo credit: Štěpán Bartoš

Photo credit: Štěpán Bartoš

Having seen his book, *Minimum*, the monks of the Cistercian Order commissioned John Pawson to design a new monastery from the remains of a derelict Baroque manor house and associated farm buildings in Bohemia. The design aimed to remain true to the spirit of St Bernard's twelfth century architectural blueprint for the Order, with its emphasis on the quality of light and proportion – on simple, pared down elevations and detailing.

A single level cloister links the various old and new buildings whilst negotiating a steep change in level across the site. A continuous window wraps around three sides of the courtyard, unbroken by structural supports or glazing mullions.

The roof and upper wall of the cloister are supported on a series of propped steel rafters from which a steel edge channel is suspended. The vault is formed from thin plasterboard bent over a frame of aluminium bearers hung from the steel structure. The window frames are concealed with only black silicone vertical joints between panes. At the corners two 400 mm width sealed units have been mitre-cut at 45° and glued together to form an almost invisible joint.

The window sill is coloured pre-cast concrete made to appear like a single monolithic piece running from inside to outside. The sill acts as a continuous window seat internally with concealed lighting beneath to wash the floor with sufficient light for circulation. Externally the sill becomes a drainage trough. There are no gutters or downpipes on the cloister roof so rainwater pours off the edges into the trough. Raised drainage outlets ensure the trough stays full at a constant level without overflowing and the trough is emptied in the winter to prevent damage from freezing water. The water bounces sunlight up onto the curved ceiling filling the cloister with shimmering reflections.

Photo credit: Štěpán Bartoš

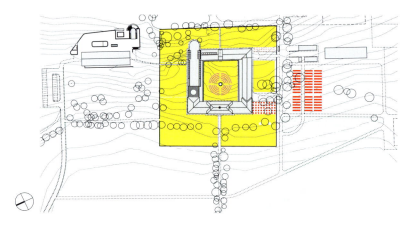

Site plan, scale 1:4000

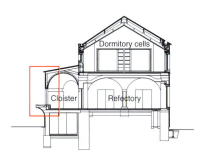

Section through south wing with area of detail shown in red, scale 1:400

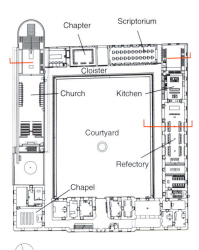

Plan, scale 1:1500

Section through east wing, scale 1:1500

1. Roof
Titanium-zinc sheet 0.7 mm thick.
Bituminous isolating layer.
18 mm WBP plywood.
Ventilated cold roof void.

2. Roof structure
200 mm deep steel I-section rafters with 200 mm deep steel I-section props fixed to new steel frame of first floor dormitories.
160 × 65 mm steel channel hangers.
160 × 65 mm steel channel beam at head of glazed opening.

3. Cloister ceiling
Matt off-white emulsion paint finish.
3 mm plaster skim coat.
One-layer 9 mm plasterboard fixed at 200 mm centres to bearers to form curved soffit with taped and filled joints.
Mineral wool insulation.
Sixteen 45 × 15 mm galvanised steel channel section bearers running along length of cloister at 400 mm centres fixed to curved channels.
Curved galvanised steel channel sections hung from primary steelwork on galvanised hanger brackets at 600 mm centres.

4. External wall (high level)
Acrylic render with plastic reinforcing mesh.
10 mm thick calcium-silicate board.
Timber battens fixed to steel frame.

5. Continuous window
Acrylic render with plastic reinforcing mesh on 10 mm thick calcium-silicate board to form reveal with 15 mm continuous ventilation gap next to glass.
65 × 69 × 3 mm concealed aluminium head channel.
1780 mm high × 2400 mm length double-glazed sealed units with 8 mm toughened inner, 20 mm cavity, 8 mm toughened outer.

Black silicone joints between adjacent panes.
65 × 40 × 3 mm concealed drained aluminium sill channel.
60 × 24 mm steel channel to pack frame up off concrete plinth.

6. Floor
3–4 mm thick buff coloured satin finish epoxy self-levelling resin floor finish.
85 mm sand–cement screed laid over underfloor heating pipes.
Polythene sheet separating layer.
65 mm rigid insulation.
300 mm reinforced concrete slab.
15 mm plaster finish to soffit below.

7. Seat
Pre-cast honey-colour pigmented concrete bench in 3 m lengths with 390 × 100 mm top and 260 × 70 mm downstand.
Continuous reinforced concrete support cast off floor slab.
Continuous low intensity strip lighting concealed beneath bench.

8. Trough
1220 mm wide by maximum 320 mm deep pre-cast honey-colour pigmented concrete trough in 3 m lengths acting as gutter and reflecting pool.
Continuous reinforced concrete upstand to slab edge to support trough.
Overflow drain to maintain water at constant level.

9. External wall (low level)
Acrylic render with plastic reinforcing mesh.
95 mm expanded polystyrene insulation adhesive fixed to blockwork.
440 mm width load-bearing wall made from hollow terracotta blockwork.
15 mm plaster internal finish.

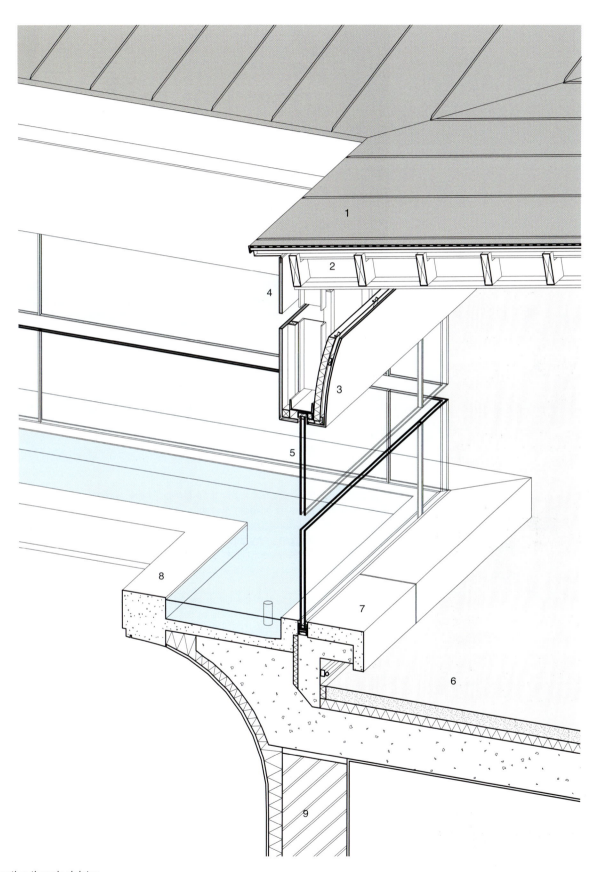

Section though cloister

Summerhouse, Stoke Newington, London

Architect: Ullmayer Sylvester Architects
Structural Engineer: BTA Structural Design

The summerhouse sits beneath mature trees at the end of a 45 × 6.5 m east – west orientated garden. A steel structure of 152 × 152 mm I-sections spans between concrete pad foundations to make a raised deck, with ventilation beneath to carry the floor. Softwood joists span between the steels with insulation in between. Birch-faced plywood floor panels are fixed down to the joists, cut to accentuate the splay of the plan.

To achieve good edges on the birch-faced plywood floor and wall cladding, 100 mm has been cut off each side of the standard 1220 mm sheets to make 1000 mm wide sheets. The floor joists and 94 × 45 mm studwork walls have been built at 500 m centres instead of 600 mm to suit the cut-down sheets.

The polycarbonate roof is fixed in a patent glazing system to timber joists. At the perimeter an aluminium channel is fixed to the polycarbonate with clear silicone.

Only the floor is insulated and there are no vapour barriers since the structure is only for summer occupation. The south side is clad in 18 mm WBP plywood, painted to reduce glare in the neighbouring garden. The north side has been clad in an additional layer of 18 mm plywood, which was cut to size on site and then taken to a workshop where stainless steel sheets were cut precisely to fit the templates. The stainless steel was glued to the plywood and then the sheets fixed back in place on site, offset 500 mm from the first plywood layer. The 3 mm joints are filled with clear silicone. The stainless steel sheets have a bright annealed finish, considerably cheaper than the slightly more reflective mirror polished finish.

Photo credit: Kilian O'Sullivan/VIEW

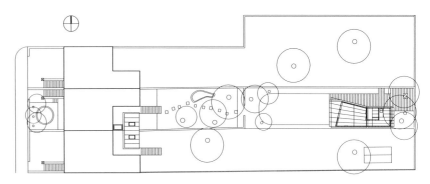

Site plan, scale 1:500

The east and west ends are single-glazed. A tool shed divides the summerhouse into two rooms. The main one looks back down the garden to the house while the smaller one is more intimate facing the mature tree trunks. The space adjacent to the summerhouse is contained by a crank in the mirrored wall, which turns the shady pathway into a secret garden.

East–west section, scale 1:200

1. Foundations
Eight 750 × 750 × 300 mm thick concrete pad foundations.

2. Steelwork
Eight 250 mm high 152 × 152 mm UC (universal column) steel posts.
152 × 152 mm UC steel beams spanning between posts.

3. Timber floor
200 × 50 mm softwood joists at 500 mm centres.
50 × 50 mm softwood noggins nailed to sides of joists.
75 mm thick rigid foil-backed insulation between joists.

4. Floor finish
18 mm birch-faced WBP plywood screwed to joists at 200 mm centres in nominal 500 mm widths, widening to 750 mm width at west end.
18 mm birch-faced marine plywood decking externally.

5. North wall
94 × 45 mm vertical softwood studs at 500 mm centres with horizontal 94 × 45 mm noggins at 600 mm centres.

6. Mirror cladding to north wall
18 mm WBP plywood sheathing in 1000 mm width sheets.
18 mm WBP plywood external sheathing in 1000 mm width sheets offset 500 mm from inner layer.
Bright annealed stainless steel sheet in 1000 mm widths glued to outer layer of plywood.

7. South wall
94 × 45 mm vertical softwood studs at 500 mm centres with horizontal 94 × 45 mm noggins at 600 mm centres.

18 mm WBP plywood external sheathing in 1000 mm width sheets with painted finish externally.

8. Internal tool shed wall
94 × 45 mm vertical softwood studs at 500 mm centres with horizontal 94 × 45 mm noggins at 600 mm centres.
18 mm birch-faced WBP plywood sheathing in 1000 mm width sheets to shed side of studwork.
18 mm birch-faced WBP plywood sheathing in 1000 mm width sheets packed off inside of studwork at 6° angle to conceal fluorescent batten light fittings.

9. Glazed screen at east and west ends
194 × 94 mm softwood frame with two vertical 194 × 45 mm mullions.
Glazed softwood door made up from 144 × 57 mm members on bottom rail and jamb containing mortice latch and 94 × 57 mm members on other two sides.
6 mm toughened single glazing to door and fixed panes.

10. Roof
200 × 50 mm softwood joists at nominal 500 mm centres, widening to 730 mm centres at west end fixed to 5° fall.
200 mm wide central gutter formed from 200 × 50 mm joist laid on its side with one-piece aluminium top-hat section gutter fixed to tops of joists.
Aluminium patent glazing channels fixed to joists.
16 mm double wall clear polycarbonate cut from 6000 × 1250 mm sheets.
Aluminium channel trim fixed to exposed edges of polycarbonate with clear silicone.

11. External works
Softwood decking to path adjacent to summerhouse.
Gravel over ground with void for free air circulation beneath summerhouse.

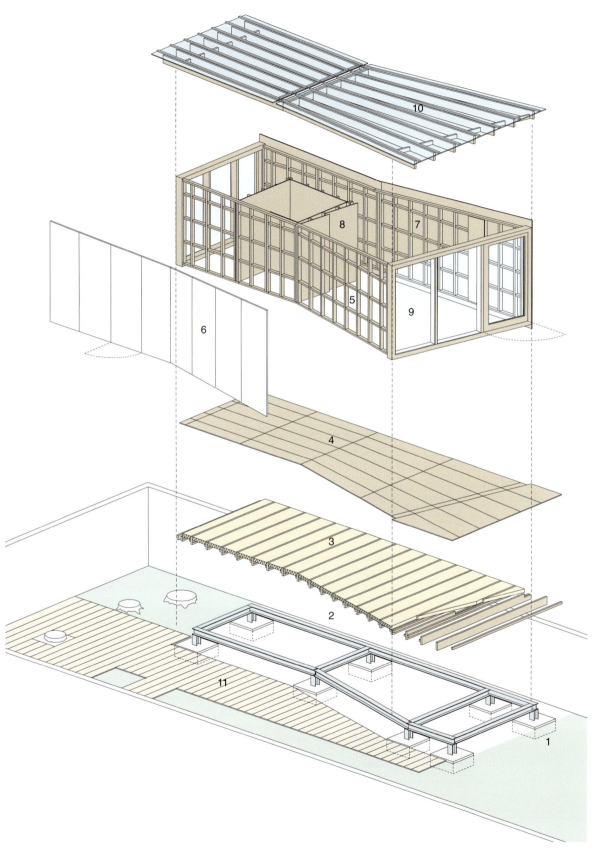

Exploded view of summerhouse

Photo credit: Edmund Sumner/VIEW

Photo credit: London bloc

Photo credit: London bloc

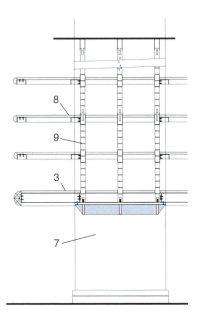

Detail section through end of static
unit, scale 1:30

Imperial War Museum Visitors Centre Duxford, Cambridgeshire

Architect: London Bloc Architects
Shell Refurbishment Architect: HOK

The historic First and Second World War airfield at Duxford is home to a large collection of civil and military aircraft. The visitors centre is the entrance and the exit of a visit to the aviation museum. The building, a Second World War era armoury, was refurbished to shell standard by HOK. The same space operates in two modes simultaneously, as a ticket sales and introduction space on the way in and as a shop on the way out. The entrance procedure has to cope with very high peak flows so is simple and direct while the exit route is more labyrinthine.

A series of folded wing-like display units are arranged to encourage circulation through the shop. From a heavy base at one end the units lift off the floor and hang from existing concrete columns on concealed steel plate brackets. The display units are welded together from galvanised mild steel channels and clad in 18 mm MDF screw fixed to the steel carcass from behind. Brushed aluminium effect laminate has been high pressure bonded to all exposed surfaces, taken round the ends at a 60 mm radius by clamping a negative mould over the laminate as it was glued to bull-nose formers. Inset shelves and display compartments are painted sky blue inside and concealed fluorescent tubes beneath the units are sheathed with filters to give out a blue glow.

Clear 5 mm acrylic has been used for inset boxes in the recessed compartments for ease of cleaning. Places have been provided for price labels by routing a recess in the MDF surface and inserting a clear acrylic cover which sits flush with the surface.

At the narrow end of the unit adjustable shelves are supported on three aluminium poles. Compression rings in the shelves engage with regular grooves in the poles holding them in place.

Photo credit: Edmund Sumner/VIEW

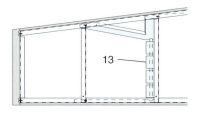

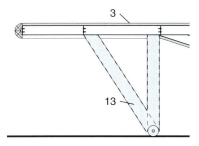

Detail section through end of mobile unit, scale 1:30

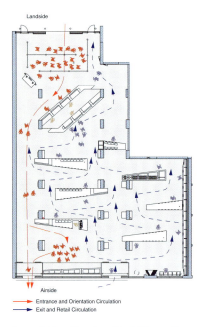

Layout plan showing circulation pattern

1. Plinth
100 × 50 × 3 mm galvanised cold rolled steel channel sections welded together to form plinth resting on floor.
100 × 18 mm MDF fascia panels with brushed aluminium effect laminate screw fixed from behind.
Removable panel on one side front-fixed to allow access to floor box.

2. Carcass
76 × 38 × 3 mm galvanised cold rolled steel channel sections welded together to form carcass.
Carcass welded to plinth.

3. Top and side surfaces
Brushed aluminium effect laminate high pressure bonded to 18 mm MDF.
Longitudinal edges formed by overlapping top layer of laminate over side panel.
60 mm radius ends formed by gluing and clamping laminate around softwood formers.

4. Recessed shelves
18 mm MDF shelf and rear panel fixed to carcass from behind and painted with sky blue polyurethane paint to resist impact.

5. Recessed compartments
Seven 400 × 200 × 94 mm deep recessed display compartments formed from 18 mm MDF painted sky blue and screw-fixed to carcass from behind.
376 × 194 × 94 mm insert boxes made from 5 mm clear high impact acrylic.

6. Pricing strips
150 × 40 × 4 mm clear acrylic strips with two countersunk screw holes set into recess in MDF to sit flush with surface.
114 × 40 × 6 mm recess in MDF below acrylic strip for price label.
Two 8 mm diameter glue-in dowels to take M4 stainless steel fixing screws for acrylic strip.

7. Existing column
970 × 425 mm existing concrete column.
12.5 mm plasterboard fixed to all sides and forming new duct for services.
Mild steel support bracket with 745 × 550 × 15 mm top plate bolted to underside of display unit.

8. Suspended shelves
Two 1750 mm length × 56 mm thick shelves tapering from 713 mm to 500 mm width.
One 2000 mm length × 56 mm thick shelf tapering from 794 mm to 500 mm width.
Shelf carcass formed from 76 × 38 × 3 mm galvanised cold rolled steel channel sections bolted together on their sides.
56 × 28 mm softwood bull-nose end formers.
18 mm MDF with brushed aluminium effect laminate surface high pressure bonded to all faces and bull-nose ends.

9. Shelf support poles
Three aluminium shelf support poles screwed to steel bracket below and screwed to concrete soffit above.
Adjustable height shelves held in place by rubber compression rings fitting into grooves in poles.

10. Sloping soffit
18 mm MDF with brushed aluminium effect laminate surface high pressure bonded to sloping underside of carcass.
100 × 94 mm recess formed in underside of soffit with 18 mm painted MDF for concealed light.
Two 1200 mm length IP65 sleeved fluorescent strip lights fixed into recess.
Blue colour filter bonded to underside and reflective strip bonded to top side of fluorescent strip lamp.

11. Floor
New reinforced concrete floor.
12 mm cementitious screed finish.

12. Floor box
442 × 440 mm floor box providing electrical and data connections to display unit.

13. Leg for mobile unit
Triangular frame welded up from 80 × 40 mm RHSs (rolled hollow sections).
Nylon rollers on steel bar between frames.

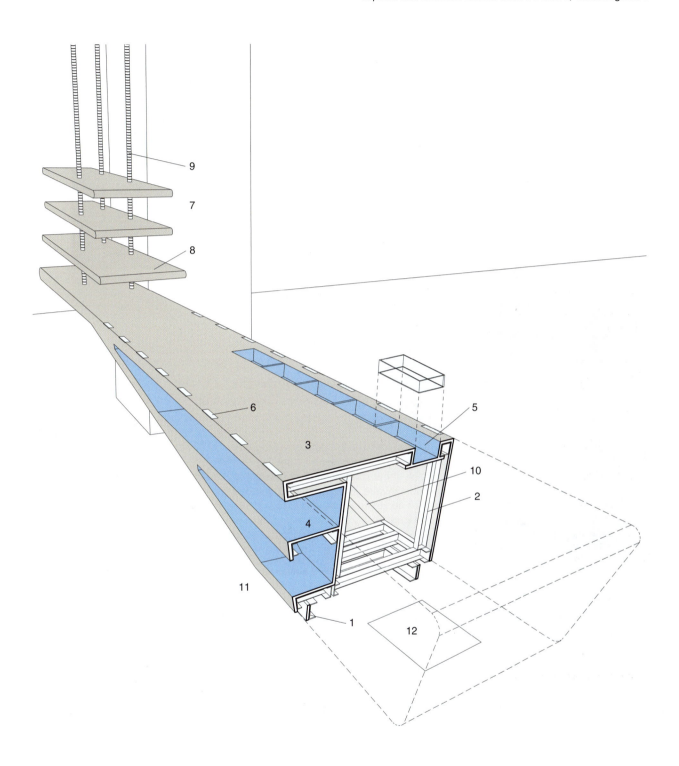

Section through typical display unit

Photo credit: Hélène Binet

Photo credit: Keith Williams Architects

Photo credit: Keith Williams Architects

Photo credit: Hélène Binet

Unicorn Theatre, London

Architect: Keith Williams Architects
Structural, M & E Services Engineer: Arup

The Unicorn Theatre puts on a programme of professional productions for children aged between four and twelve years old. Its new base on the South Bank of the Thames has a 350-seat main auditorium suspended over a 120-seat studio theatre. A 1000 mm deep ribbed concrete slab spanning 18 m forms the main auditorium floor, supported on three sides by 400 mm thick load-bearing reinforced concrete walls on concrete piles. Above first floor level the walls reduce to 300 mm thick and form a structural box cantilevering out over the foyer below.

On the south side of the auditorium above the main public staircase is a second volume containing an education room and plant room. At the east end the steel structure sits on concrete piers but, to avoid the need for columns in the foyer below, the west end is hung from the auditorium structure. The floors are 275 mm thick concrete slabs on profiled steel decking spanning between 254 × 254 mm steel beams. On the north side the beams sit, isolated by neoprene acoustic bearings, on a 200 × 200 mm angle bolted to the auditorium wall.

On the south side the floor beams are carried by deep beams supported at the foyer end by a diagonal hanger. The hanger is a 203 × 203 mm steel I-section with a T-shaped bracket bolted to the top. To maintain acoustic separation the connection to the auditorium wall is made as a compression joint even though the hanger itself is in tension. The T-bracket hooks through a hanger bracket cast into the auditorium wall where it rests on a neoprene acoustic bearing in between.

All plant has acoustic attenuation and sits on neoprene isolation pads to prevent noise transfer into the auditorium. The education room is lined with a sprung timber floor, acoustic plasterboard ceiling and plastered blockwork walls, separated from the concrete auditorium wall by a cavity.

The suspended volume is clad in insulated render. The glazing of the foyer has 220 mm deep horizontal mullions and glass-to-glass vertical joints to minimise the amount of vertical structure and emphasise the floating nature of the boxes hanging above.

Photo credit: Hélène Binet

Photo credit: Hélène Binet

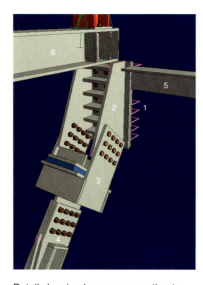

Detail showing hanger connection to auditorium wall

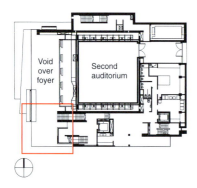

Mezzanine level plan with area of detail shown in red, scale 1:750

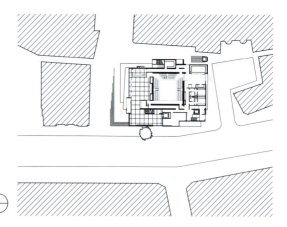

Site plan, scale 1:1500

1. Wall plate
800 × 500 × 25 mm thick plate with fifteen bolt holes cast into auditorium concrete wall. Steel U-bars and 100 mm long × 19 mm diameter shear studs welded to rear of plate to provide anchor into concrete.

2. Wall bracket
800 × 500 × 25 mm thick back plate bolted to cast-in wall plate with fifteen M24 bolts. Two 1000 × 600 × 25 mm thick shaped plates welded to back plate with stiffening plates welded in between.

3. Hanger bracket
500 × 600 × 25 mm thick side plates bolted to wall bracket with twelve M24 bolts each side. 650 × 400 × 25 mm thick plate bearer with 25 mm stiffening plates welded to side plates.

4. Hanger
650 × 300 × 25 mm thick plate with 25 mm stiffening plates bearing on rubber acoustic bearing.
500 × 500 × 25 mm thick plate welded to bearer.
Two 800 × 500 × 25 mm tapered plates bolted to T-bearer with twelve M24 bolts.
203 × 203 mm × 86 kg UC (universal column) hanger welded to tapered plates.

5. Bracket for floor beams
200 × 200 × 16 mm equal angle fixed to auditorium wall with 2 rows anchor bolts at 200 mm centres.
Resilient foam strip between angle and concrete to prevent structure-to-structure contact.

6. Floor beam
254 × 254 mm × 107 kg UC floor beams at nominal 2010 mm centres bolted to bracket on rubber acoustic bearing isolated with neoprene sleeves and washers.

7. Auditorium wall
300 mm thick reinforced concrete wall. Cavity filled with mineral wool insulation. 140 mm concrete blockwork. 10 mm plaster finish to education room only.

8. Roof
300 mm thick concrete slab on permanent metal deck.
100 mm extruded polystyrene insulation. Single-ply roofing membrane.
50 mm thick concrete pavers on 20 mm gravel over plant area.

9. External walls
Acrylic render external finish.
80 mm expanded polystyrene insulation.
20 mm cementitious board backing on metal studwork frame on south elevation only where blockwork is set back to conceal hanger.
140 mm concrete blockwork.
10 mm plaster internal finish.

10. Education room floor
Sprung battened timber floating floor.
275 mm concrete slab on profiled metal decking.
Two layers plasterboard ceiling on resilient acoustic hangers.

11. Floor end beam
533 × 210 mm × 109 kg UB (universal beam) end compression member.

12. Auditorium balcony structure
Diagonal concrete corner brace to resist compression force from floor end beam built into auditorium balcony structure.

13. Foyer glazing
Frameless sealed double-glazed units with 220 mm deep aluminium horizontal mullions suspended on 20 mm vertical steel rods.

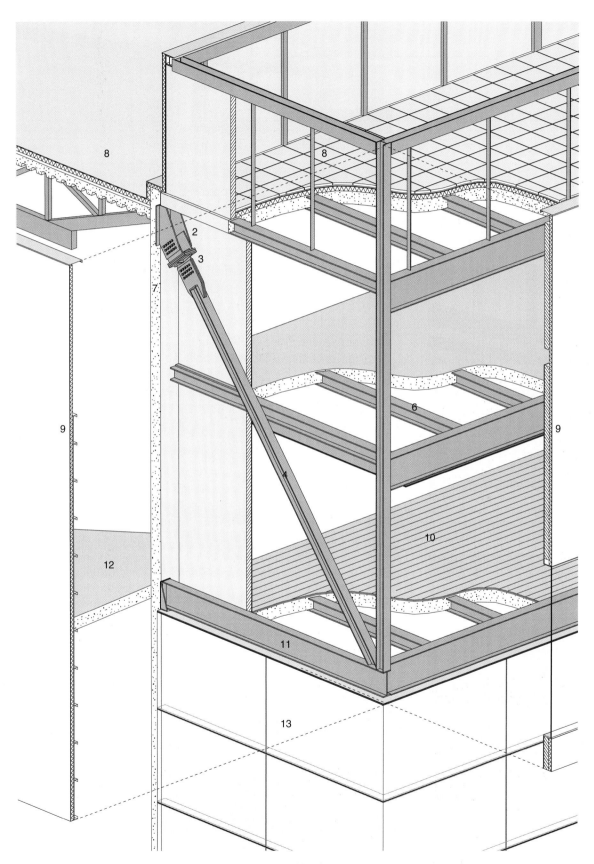

Exploded view of suspended education and plant block on south side of auditorium

Photo credit: Hélène Binet

Museum of World Culture, Gothenburg, Sweden

Architect: Brisac Gonzalez Architects
Glazing Consultant: Akiboye Conolly Architects

Photo credit: Hélène Binet

Photo credit: Hélène Binet

Won in a competition in 1999, the £26 million Museum of World Culture was Brisac Gonzalez's first building. Located on a strip of land between a major road and a steep wooded hill it brings together a number of different ethnographic collections previously housed in Gothenburg and Stockholm.

On the roadside a severe rendered grey mass looms over the road while at the rear a five-storey glazed atrium rises over the ground floor staircase. The atrium glazing is designed for maximum transparency with the minimum of vertical interruption to the panoramic view up the wooded hillside behind.

Large 4 × 2 m frameless double-glazed units are used in horizontal orientation with glass fins supporting the vertical edges. Purpose-made extruded aluminium transom 'blades' connected into the horizontal glazing joints with stainless steel rods transfer wind loads back to the vertical glass fins. The set-back between the transoms and the glass allows blinds and warm air to pass and makes the structure appear lighter. The glass fins span 6 m between primary steel beams. At this length glass fins normally have to be made in shorter sections and bolted together with heavy splice plates which are clumsy and visually intrusive.

Using 6 m lengths of glass it is possible to make the fins in ordinary laminated annealed glass without joints. The problem with laminated annealed glass is in making connections to it – the concentrated stresses applied in bolted fixings will cause cracking. Here the transom is bolted to a 200 mm diameter toughened glass patch, which is then bonded to the laminated fin. The bond distributes the load at low stress into the fin. At the top and bottom the glass fin is bonded to steel shoes, which are bolted to tongues welded to the steel beams. The glass is not clamped but transfers load in shear through the adhesive bond.

The inner pane is untinted laminated low-E glass. The outer pane is toughened, incorporating sensors connected to the intruder alarm by wires hidden in the vertical joints. Internal translucent aluminised fabric blinds allow the atrium walls to be used for projection after dark.

Photo credit: Hélène Binet

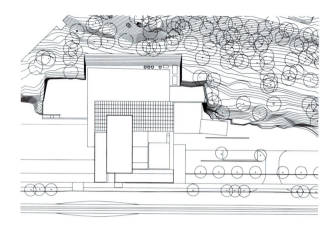

Site plan, scale 1:2000

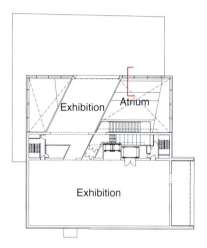

Second floor plan with area of detail
shown in red, scale 1:1000

Section through atrium

1. Steel structure
400 × 400 mm square hollow section steel
primary beams at nominal 6 m centres vertically.

2. Glass fin
5600 × 780 mm glass fin made from two sheets
10 mm thick annealed glass with bevelled
edges.
780 × 100 × 10 mm tapered steel plates
bonded to either side of fin with polyvinylbutyral
(PVB) curing adhesive and bolted to 20 mm
thick steel tongue welded to primary beam.
Extruded aluminium channel profile factory
bonded to outside edge of fin with PVB curing
adhesive.
Cables for intruder alarm concealed in slots in
extruded edge channel.

3. Glass patch
200 mm diameter × 15 mm thick polished
toughened glass patch with bevelled edge
factory bonded to glass fin with PVB curing
adhesive.

4. Connector
80 mm diameter × 18 mm thick polished
stainless steel connector bolted to glass patch
with M16 countersunk stainless steel bolt.
Dense fibre washer between patch and
connector.
80 × 60 × 10 mm thick polished stainless steel
lug welded to connector with slotted hole.

5. Transom
3700 × 140 × 60 mm purpose-made extruded
aluminium transom.

Continuous threaded channel in transom to
take wind ties.

6. End plate
140 × 60 × 5 mm polished stainless steel end
plate screwed to end of transom with M10
bolts.
Two 80 × 60 × 10 mm thick polished stainless
steel lugs welded to end plate.
M10 pan-head bolt connection between end
plate and connector.

7. Connection to glass
200 mm length × 16 mm diameter stainless
steel wind ties screwed into continuous
threaded channel in transom at 1000 mm
centres.
Stainless steel toggle screwed to end of wind
tie slotted into horizontal glazing joint and
rotated 90° to clamp glazing.

8. Glazing
4 × 2 m sealed double-glazed unit with 8 mm
toughened outer pane, 16 mm argon filled cavity
and 8.8 mm laminated low-E inner pane.
Aluminium Z-profile spacers to take toggle
fixings from wind ties.

9. Blinds
Translucent aluminised fabric roller blinds fixed
to steel beams.
Stainless steel cable guides fixed to steel
beams.

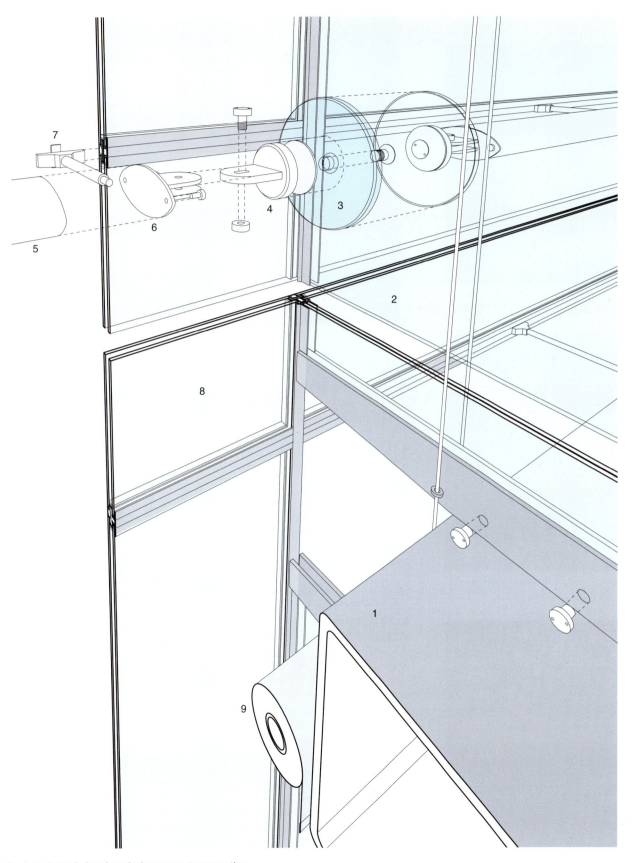

Exploded detail showing glazing support connection

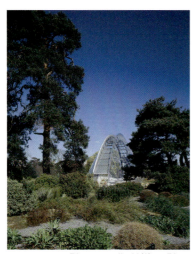

Photo credit: Hélène Binet

Photo credit: Hélène Binet

Photo credit: Hélène Binet

Alpine House
Kew Gardens, London

Architect: Wilkinson Eyre Architects
Services Engineer: Atelier Ten
Structural Engineer: Dewhurst Macfarlane & Partners

The new glass house provides a controlled environment for the Royal Botanic Gardens' Alpine plant collection using almost entirely passive systems. On the east and west sides single sheets of toughened laminated glass are clamped to 20 mm diameter stainless steel tension cables which span between two parabolic arches. The arches are solid 240×120 mm steel plates fixed to concrete plinths at each end. Two such pairs have been placed back to back forming an 8 m high enclosure. Openable vents controlled by a thermostat allow air drawn up behind the glass by stack effect to escape at the top.

At ground level air can enter below the glass through stainless steel mesh grilles that prevent ingress of vermin. By using low iron float glass visible light transmission through the laminated panes could be as high as 90%. Shading is required in warm weather to reduce heat gain and control direct sunlight on the plants. Blinds on the east, west and south sides open automatically on guide wires and are concealed behind a concrete plinth in their closed position.

A mechanical ventilation system integrated into the floor slab supplies cool airflow around the plants. The floor slab is constructed as a labyrinth of blockwork walls with a large surface area. At night air can be blown through the labyrinth to cool it down so that during the day outside air can be drawn through, cooled and released through nozzles set amongst the plants. The idea comes from the way termite mounds are constructed to draw air through the ground to cool before it passes up through the mound. A low pressure hot water coil may also be used to provide a minimal level of heating in the winter.

Photo credit: Hélène Binet

Photo credit: Hélène Binet

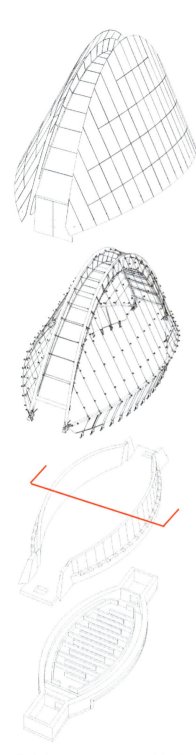

Exploded diagram with area of detail shown in red

Site plan, scale 1:1500

1. Ground Slab
350 mm reinforced concrete slab.
Sodium bentonite geotextile tanking membrane.
50 mm sand blinding.
150 mm minimum hardcore.

2. Labyrinth
500 mm high × 140 mm width concrete blockwork walls at 665 mm centres to form labyrinth with perimeter plenum on each side to cool supply air.

3. Floor
1200 mm wide × 100 mm deep pre-cast concrete planks bedded on labyrinth walls.
250 mm reinforced concrete slab on pre-cast planks.

4. Vent
100 mm diameter stainless steel air distribution vent with periscope outlet to supply cool air at low level over plants.
Heights vary from 500–700 mm.
Integral damper in vertical duct to prevent backflow.

5. Walkway
100 mm thick brick piers at maximum 2500 mm centres with stainless steel ties at 500 mm centres top and bottom.
125 mm thick reinforced concrete walkway slab spanning between piers.
150 mm thick screed.
Cold applied Macadam finish.
450 mm high curved stainless steel kicker plates bolted to both sides of slab.

6. Planting
Liquid applied bituminous tanking membrane across floor and up to top of upstand walls.
French drain formed from gravel falling to sump drain at either end.

7. Structural wall
Curved reinforced in-situ concrete wall 940 mm wide at base tapering to 260 mm at top, fair-faced finish.
Top of wall cut off at 19° angle to follow curve of truss arch.

8. Roof structure
Solid 240 × 120 mm plate curved to form parabolic structural arch fixed at both ends to concrete plinth.
16 mm diameter stainless steel rod ties at 1000 mm centres pin jointed to plates welded to top and bottom of steel arch.
Plate connection to concrete plinth at base pin jointed to lower rod tie.

9. Glazing
2000 × 1000 mm laminated glass panes made up from two layers 6 mm toughened low-iron float glass fixed to cables with six clamp plates per pane.

10. Mesh panels
Panels formed from stainless steel mesh with maximum aperture 20 mm held in 20 mm width stainless steel clamping channels on four sides.

11. Blinds
Automatic retractable blinds with tubular motors on guide wires behind approximately 80% of glazing to reflect excess solar gain in warm weather.
Blinds retract behind concrete wall when not in use.

12. External path
10 mm approximate thickness of resin bonded gravel surface to path for maintenance.
100 mm thick concrete base.
1200 gauge polythene damp-proof membrane.

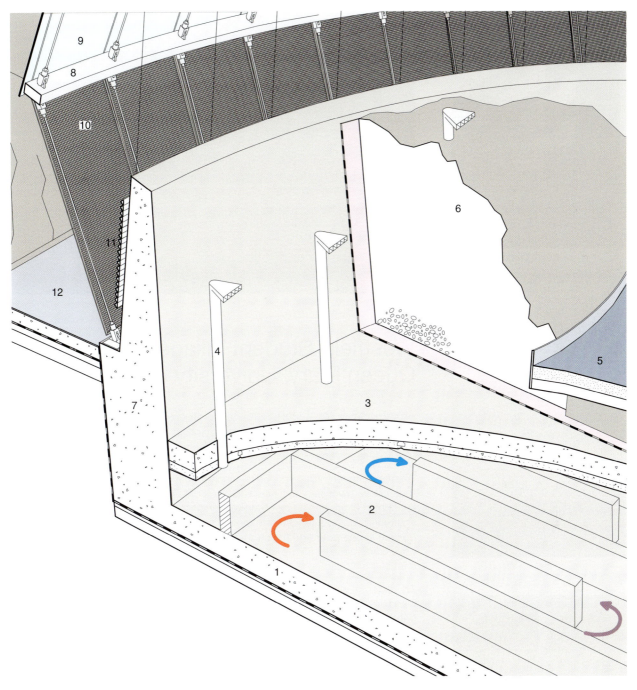

Cut-away section though floor and wall

Photo credit: Will Pryce

Photo credit: Will Pryce

Photo credit: Feilden Clegg Bradley Architects

Photo credit: Feilden Clegg Bradley Architects

Westfield Student Village, Queen Mary, University of London

Architect: Feilden Clegg Bradley Architects
Structural Engineer: Adams Kara Taylor

Westfield Student Village provides accommodation for 995 students and visitors together with ancillary facilities such as a cafè/bar and laundry. The largest residential block has an eight-storey concrete frame built with tunnel-form shuttering. Using a tunnel form means two walls and the floor of a bay can be cast in one pour and the shutter struck 24 hours later. Two 5.1 m wide bays were made at a time with other trades following on immediately behind enabling the building to be built very quickly.

The external walls have a light gauge steel (LGS) studwork frame with pre-oxidised copper cladding in non-standard 450 mm width horizontal bands to tie in with a standard window module. A false horizontal seam conceals a movement joint at each floor level.

The long north elevation is broken up by a series of projecting triangular 'flippers', the floors and roofs of which were cast as extensions to the standard tunnel form slabs. The two outside walls were poured with the following floor of tunnel forms. To avoid temporary propping reinforcement was enhanced locally to allow the slabs to cantilever until the box wall construction was complete.

The flippers have a timber studwork structure fixed to a wall plate top and bottom, requiring fewer fixings into the concrete than an LGS frame and therefore minimising cold bridging. The client demanded a higher acoustic performance than stipulated by building regulations because of the adjacent mainline railway. All north elevation windows have a third internal glazing pane and the building achieved a very good airtightness test rating.

The shorter flipper walls are clad in brushed stainless steel to relieve the darkness of the elevation. The bright east facing stainless steel ends catch the morning light while the longer copper faces glow orange in the sunset.

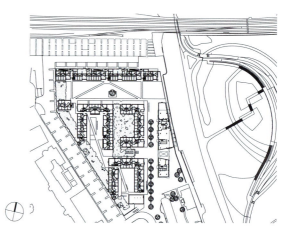

Site plan, scale 1:4000

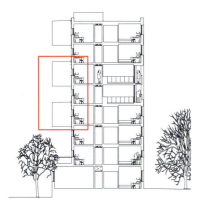

North – south section with area of
detail shown in red, scale 1:500

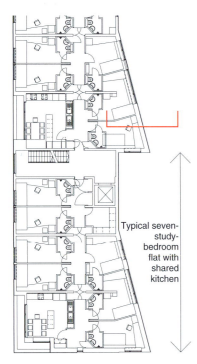

Typical seven-
study-
bedroom
flat with
shared
kitchen

Typical upper floor plan with area of
detail shown in red, scale 1:500

1. Primary Structure
200 mm thick reinforced concrete slab and
180 mm width reinforced concrete walls built
using tunnel formwork.

2. Typical external wall
Two layers 12.5 mm plasterboard internal lining
taped, jointed and painted.
30 mm dense mineral board for acoustic
insulation mounted on resilient bars.
100 mm lightweight galvanised steel studs at
600 mm centres.
65 mm rigid mineral wool insulation between
studs.
20 mm coreboard between studs.
15 mm air gap.
30 mm foil-faced rigid phenolic insulation with
all joints taped for airtightness.
60 × 18 mm tanalised plywood spacer strips at
each vertical stud.
18 mm WBP plywood fixed through spacers to
vertical metal studs.
Breather membrane.
0.7 mm gauge copper cladding with 25 mm
horizontal standing seams at 450 mm centres
with dummy seam at slab level to allow for
deflection.

3. Windows
Softwood inner window frame.
20 mm width mastic sealant joint with wall
structure.
Polyester powder coated aluminium outer sash.
Sealed double-glazed unit with 4 mm
toughened low-E inner pane, 16 mm cavity,
4 mm toughened outer pane.
4 mm toughed glass third pane in aluminium
frame mounted on window frame internally on
clips to increase acoustic insulation.

4. Floor of flipper
Carpet on self-levelling latex layer.
200 mm reinforced concrete floor slab painted
externally with bituminous DPM (damp-proof
membrane).
75 × 50 mm tanalised softwood battens fixed
to underside of slab with 30 mm packing zone
for tolerance.

75 mm rigid mineral wool insulation between
battens.
18 mm WBP plywood fixed to battens.
Breather membrane.
0.7 mm gauge grade 304 brushed stainless
steel sheet folded to form nominal 315 mm wide
15 mm deep planks with Z-profile edges.
Planks fixed with self-tapping stainless steel
screws at 1000 mm centres with butyl sealing
tape between stainless steel and plywood.
185 mm width copper edge trim at joint with
flipper external wall.

5. Roof of flipper
0.7 mm gauge copper with 25 mm single lock
standing seams at 450 mm centres.
Breather membrane.
Two layers 9.5 mm WBP plywood curved to
follow timber joists below.
100 × 50 mm tanalised softwood joists.
Ridge and eaves are at constant height so roof
pitch gets steeper as roof gets narrower.
125 mm rigid mineral wool insulation.
200 mm reinforced concrete floor slab painted
externally with bituminous DPM.
Painted concrete internal finish.

6. Flipper external wall structure
180 mm reinforced concrete wall cast in-situ
painted externally with bituminous DPM.

7. Cladding support
150 × 50 mm tanalised softwood wall plate
fixed to concrete at top and bottom of wall and
above and below windows with 20 mm packing
zone for tolerance.
125 × 75 mm tanalised timber studs fixed to
wall plates at 600 mm centres.
125 mm rigid mineral wool insulation between
studs.
18 mm WBP plywood external sheathing.
Breather membrane.

8. North wall cladding
0.7 mm gauge copper cladding with 25 mm
horizontal single lock standing seams at
450 mm centres.

Cut-away section though projecting rooms on north elevation

9. East wall cladding
0.7 mm gauge grade 304 brushed stainless steel sheet folded to form nominal 315 mm wide 15 mm deep planks with Z-profile edges. Planks fixed with self-tapping stainless steel screws at 1000 mm centres with butyl sealing tape between stainless steel and plywood.

10. Window spandrel panel
3 mm thick polyester powder coated pressed aluminium plate fixed top and bottom with self-tapping screws at 600 mm centres to plywood backing.
50 × 50 × 1 mm gauge polyester powder coated pressed aluminium angle closer fixed to plywood behind plate at window edges and head.

Photo credit: Edmund Sumner/VIEW

Carlisle Lane Housing
Waterloo, London

Architect: Pringle Richards Sharratt Architects
Timber panels and cladding: Eurban and Finnforest Merk

Tucked away behind the snaking viaduct into Waterloo Station a development of four residential units has been shoehorned into a very tight ex-industrial site using materials from renewable resources and energy-efficient construction. The whole building structure of solid timber wall and roof panels was put up in three days.

To avoid piling or more substantial foundations on the marshy ground it was decided to build a lightweight structure on a reinforced concrete raft cast on the existing ground slab. Three walls of the original warehouse building have also been retained as 'free' fire-resistant, weather-resistant, party walls.

Within these walls a structural timber shell has been constructed from prefabricated laminated solid timber panels with pre-cut window and door openings. The void between the panels and existing brickwork has been injected with mineral wool insulation.

To form the roof, 200 mm deep glulam beams have been sandwiched between a basic solid timber panel and a top sarking sheet of laminated timber. Insulation made from recycled newspaper and jute sacking fills the gaps between the beams. The depth of structure allows prefabricated pitch roof forms to span the full building width with no need for tie rods.

The roof and first floor are supported directly on the walls with compression gasket seals. Lintels over the windows are made from 400 mm deep Kerto beams – a solid timber material made by laminating and gluing 3 mm softwood veneers together at high temperature. The solid timber panels form a vapour control layer and all joins are tape sealed so the structure achieves a high degree of airtightness.

Photo credit: Eurban

Photo credit: Eurban

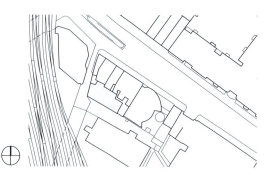

Site plan, scale 1:2000

Rigid wood-fibre insulation slabs are fixed to the external walls and Thermowood boards fixed on battens as a rainscreen. Thermowood is spruce that has been treated against decay by heating it to a temperature of 212°C to drive out the resin rather than treating it with a chemical preservative. As long as the insulation used is more vapour permeable than the timber panel, no vapour barrier is required.

The separating floors dividing the flats are built up with ballast, wood-fibre insulation and gypsum fibre-boards with a plasterboard ceiling on resilient hangers below to achieve part E Building Regulations standards. The walls are also clad in plasterboard for acoustic isolation and fire protection. On the underside of the roof the timber panels are left exposed.

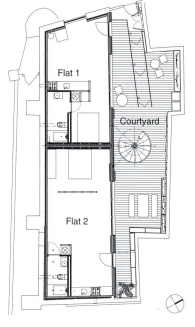

Ground floor plan, scale 1:250

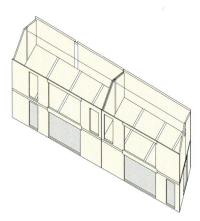

Axonometric showing timber wall and floor panels (roof not shown)

1. Ground floor
22 mm timber flooring on 2 mm jute underlay.
25 mm gypsum-fibreboard dry flooring with
60 mm extruded polystyrene bonded to rear.
200 mm reinforced concrete raft slab.
Polythene damp proof membrane.
Existing concrete slab.

2. Side boundary external wall
Two layers 12.5 mm plasterboard dry lining.
105 mm laminated timber structural panel.
Blown full-fill mineral wool insulation.
Existing rendered brickwork wall repaired.

3. Windows
Full height softwood framed windows.
Argon-filled double glazed units with low-E inner pane and laminated outer pane.

4. External wall at floor edge
400 × 105 mm glulam timber beam.
100 × 50 mm softwood studs fixed to beam.
100 mm rigid woodfibre insulation.
Breather membrane.
32 × 42 mm heat-treated softwood battens.
125 × 25 mm heat-rectified softwood tongued and grooved horizontal cladding.
92 × 21 mm heat-rectified softwood window head and reveal closer boards.
Terne-coated stainless steel cill flashing.

5. First floor
22 mm timber flooring on 2 mm jute underlay.
10 mm expansion gap at floor edges filled with mineral wool.
25 mm gypsum fibreboard dry flooring.

30 mm wood fibre resilient layer.
30 mm cardboard honeycomb filled with crushed aggregate to form ballast layer.
Acoustic membrane.
170 mm thick solid timber structural floor panel.
Two layers 12.5 mm plasterboard ceiling fixed to timber panel on resilient bars.

6. Separating wall between flats
Two layers 12.5 mm plasterboard dry lining.
75 × 50 mm softwood studwork frame on isolating bearers.
25 mm cavity.
80 mm solid timber structural wall panel.
30 mm continuous cavity filled with mineral wool isolating insulation.
80 mm solid timber structural wall panel.
25 mm cavity.
75 × 50 mm softwood studwork frame on isolating bearers.
Two layers 12.5 mm plasterboard dry lining.

7. Roof
Prefabricated structural roof panels formed from 80 mm solid timber with 200 × 80 mm glulam beams at 645 mm centres and 27 mm Kerto sarking board.
200 mm recycled newspaper and jute insulation.
Geotextile isolation layer.
Terne coated stainless steel roofing.

8. Deck
140 × 28 mm timber decking on 150 × 50 mm treated softwood joists on brickwork dwarf walls.

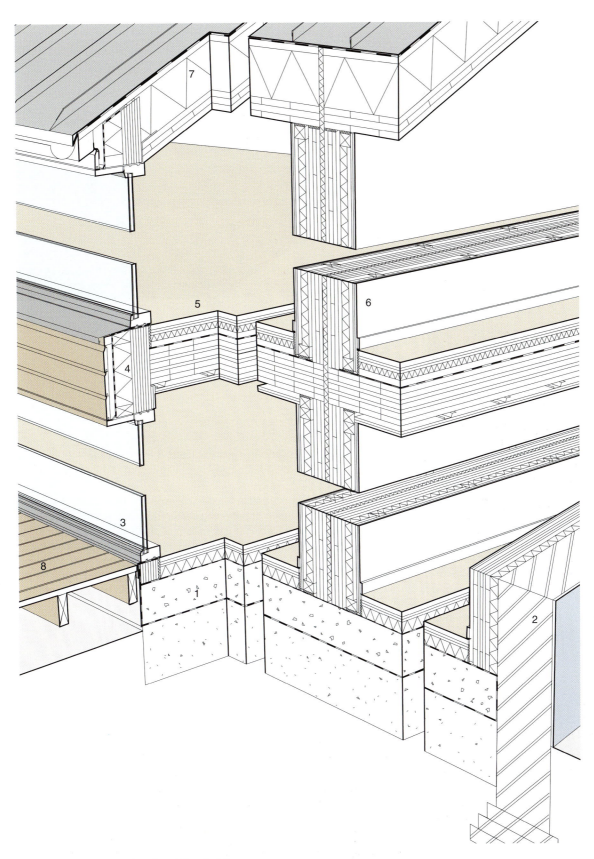

Cut-away section showing roof, wall and floor build-up

National Gallery East Wing, London

Architect: Dixon Jones Architects
Structural Engineer: Alan Baxter & Associates
M & E Services Engineer: Andrew Reid & Partners

Dixon Jones was appointed in 1998 to develop a master plan for the National Gallery with the intention of providing better front of house facilities. In the first phase of work, which cost £17 million, a disabled access route from a new public entrance on Trafalgar Square has been burrowed through the labyrinth of ground floor rooms to connect with the gallery's central circulation spaces. The main event on the route is the Annenberg Court, once an external courtyard, that has been cleared out and covered with an ETFE roof.

The walls along the route are clad to varying heights with a wainscot of Noir Saint Laurent marble, a deep chocolate-brown stone with strong white veining. The stones for each wall were quarried in France and cut in Italy where they were laid out on the floor of the stone warehouse to ensure consistency and then numbered for transportation. Each stone is individually supported on stainless steel dowels with 2 mm joints left open, so no movement joints are required.

Much of the rainwater from the gallery roofs falls towards the courtyard dropping down through 20 rainwater pipes to a holding tank and drain beneath the floor. To conceal the rainwater pipes a framework of light gauge steel channels supports the courtyard lining forming a zone for supply air ductwork and acting as a return air plenum. Cool conditioned air is supplied at low level beneath the balcony and at mid-height via 50 jet nozzles through holes cut in the top row of stones.

The upper walls and sloping ceilings of the courtyard are lined with 15 mm thick fibrous plaster panels, chosen by the subcontractor, rather than skimmed plasterboard for the guaranteed high quality finish. A curved cornice profile at the top contains fibre optic light fittings which wash light

Photo credit: Morley von Sternberg

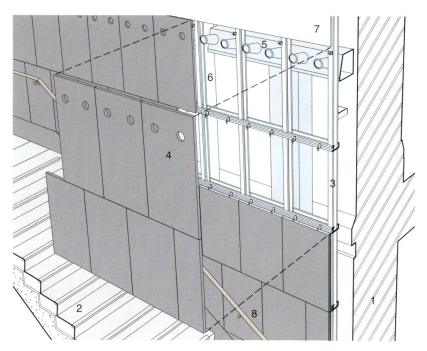

Cut-away section through stair

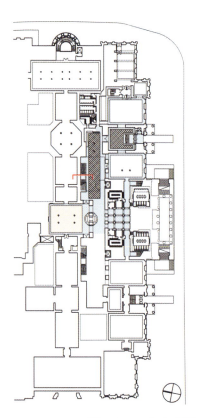

Site plan, scale 1: 1500

evenly down the ceiling planes. Cables run out to projectors mounted in stainless steel enclosures on an external steel walkway gantry cantilevered off the main roof structure. The roof light is sized to the maximum width of a single ETFE cushion. As well as being lighter and cheaper than structural glazing, ETFE can span the whole opening with no glazing bars or divisions. The curved cornice hides the roof light clamps so from below there appears to be nothing between the courtyard and the clouds passing overhead.

1. Courtyard wall
Existing external brickwork wall to courtyard.

2. Staircase
335 × 174 mm solid Azul Cascais stone tread with 50 × 25 mm contrasting Nero Belgio marble nosing stopping 100 mm short of ends. 30 mm sand–cement bed.
225 mm minimum reinforced concrete staircase structure cast in-situ.
152 × 152 mm UC (universal column) section steel beams below staircase landing encased with 15 mm glassroc frameless encasement to provide 1 hour's fire protection.

3. Steel wall lining structure
100 × 50 mm galvanised steel channels at 560 mm centres vertically and 885 mm centres horizontally built off concrete floor and staircase structure and restrained to courtyard wall with galvanised brackets allowing for vertical differential movement.

4. Stone cladding
Nominal 885 × 560 × 30 mm thick Noir Saint Laurent marble slabs hung individually from steel structure with doweled stainless steel support brackets in continuous slot channel. 2 mm open joints between stones to allow for movement.

5. Supply air ductwork
250 × 175 mm galvanised steel horizontal ducts in 2 m lengths approximately to fit between rainwater pipes.
250 × 150 mm insulated galvanised steel vertical ducts from plant room below floor to each horizontal duct.
200 mm length nozzles tapering to 80 mm diameter aperture welded to horizontal ducts at 280 mm centres.
Nozzles fitted into holes in stone cladding and sealed with black silicone.

6. Other services
Rainwater pipes from roof level gutter to holding tank in basement.
Voids between ducts and rainwater pipes form plenum for return air to basement plant room.

7. Wall and ceiling lining
Nominal 2000 × 1000 × 15 mm thick fibrous plaster panels tied to steelwork behind.

8. Handrail
54 × 20 mm bronze handrail on 20 mm diameter bronze brackets slotted over steel spigot rod welded to plate bolted to steel frame.

9. Cornice
Fibrous plaster cornice moulding tied to steelwork behind.
Fibre optic light fittings at 300 mm centres.

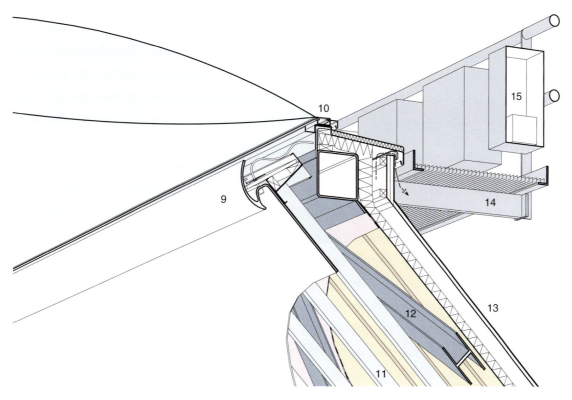

Cut-away section through ceiling and rooflight

10. Roof light
One-piece ETFE cushion held in continuous aluminium extruded clamp fixed down to steel angle.

11. Ceiling lining structure
Self-supporting framework of 100 × 50 mm galvanised steel channels at 560 mm centres independent of main steel roof structure.

12. Roof steelwork
300 × 300 mm SHS (square hollow section) ring beam around four sides of roof light opening.
152 × 152 mm UC section diagonal steel members supporting ring beam.
Continuous 200 × 100 mm steel angle welded to ring beam to support ETFE clamps.

13. Roof
175 × 50 mm treated softwood joists fixed to steel frame.
Vapour barrier fixed to underside of joists.
100 mm mineral wool insulation between joists with continuous ventilation gap above.

25 mm WBP plywood.
Standing seam lead roof covering on isolating layer.
PVC coated coping with insulated core.

14. Maintenance gantry
150 × 50 mm galvanised RHS (rolled hollow section) steel bracket cantilevered off ring beam.
100 × 75 mm galvanised steel angles supporting 30 mm deep galvanised steel walkway.
76 mm diameter galvanised CHS (circular hollow section) steel handrails spanning between 70 × 12 mm galvanised steel flat supports at 3 m centres.

15. Projector housing
Stainless steel IP rated enclosure housing fibre optic projector clamped to handrails.
Holes in base for ventilation and cable access.

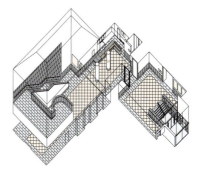

Axonometric of eastern entrance

Redshift Photography 2006

Redshift Photography 2006

National Assembly for Wales, Cardiff

Architects: Richard Rogers Partnership
Structural Engineer: Arup
Environmental Engineer: BDSP

The Welsh Assembly is a modest sized building standing next to some much bigger neighbours on the quayside on Cardiff Bay. A dramatic undulating roof projects up to 15 m beyond the footprint to give the building a bigger scale, and symbolises the Assembly reaching to the rest of Wales.

The roof is a six bay steel structure held up on 12 circular columns. The rugby ball profile of each 41.5×12 m bay is formed by two inclined steel arches held in place at an angle of 45° with secondary beams and bracing. The roof deck is galvanised steel with mineral wool insulation and an aluminium top sheet with standing seams, supplied in tapered lengths to fit the profile over the domed sections.

Natural light is reflected down to the 60-seat debating chamber from a roof light above a huge funnel of steelwork that hangs down from the roof arches. The surfaces directly below the roof light are clad in mirror polished stainless steel sheet and the funnel is lined with curved aluminium tubes to diffuse and bounce light around, eliminating direct glare.

The conical roof light is framed with steel glazing bars spanning from an oval ring beam at the base to a circular ring beam at the top. To make up the geometry the glazing is broken into triangular facets with a prismatic interlayer to further diffuse the light. An inverted 2.6 m diameter mirror polished stainless steel cone reflects light downwards and is lowered to floor level for a daily polish. For presentations in the chamber the light level can be adjusted by lowering the cone down to the narrowest point of the funnel to block out most of the light.

A wind cowl mounted above the roof light contains a bank of fixed louvres. The cowl rotates in the wind like the top of an oast house so that the louvres

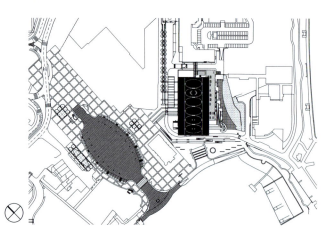

Site plan, scale 1:5000

face the leeward side. A combination of stack effect and negative pressure created by the cowl draws stale air up from the debating chamber. Below the cowl the circular roof light soffit is divided into four opening segments known as 'quadrant dampers'. These are controlled by the building management system (BMS) to regulate airflow. The roof form has been generated by a fusion of services, structural and architectural desires.

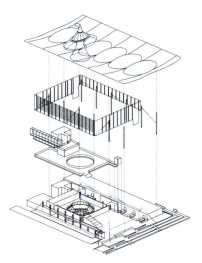

Exploded axonometric

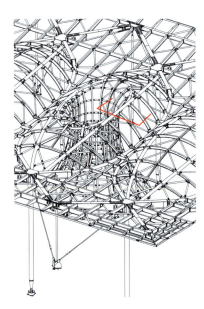

Steel structure of bay over debating chamber with area of detail shown in red

1. Structural steelwork
324 × 8 mm CHS (circular hollow section) arch spanning between columns.
219 × 8 mm CHS oval ring beam around perimeter of funnel welded to arch.
254 × 146 mm × 37 kg curved UBs (universal beams) giving lateral stability to ring beam.
Funnel structure of 254 × 146 mm × 37 kg curved UBs hung from ring beam.

2. Main roof areas
Curved galvanised steel deck spanning between steel beams.
Vapour barrier.
250 mm mineral wool insulation.
Curved aluminium standing seam roof finish.

3. Funnel lining
80 mm diameter matt anodised curved aluminium tubes with 30% free area between tubes.
30 mm thick curved acoustic absorption panels with black quilted finish on front.
Two layers 12.5 mm plasterboard fixed to curve on timber battens at 300 mm centres.
100 mm mineral wool acoustic insulation to prevent sound break-in.

4. Perimeter lining
Mirror polished stainless steel sheet lining perforated for acoustic absorption.
75 mm air gap with service run for electrical cables.
75 mm acoustic absorption insulation.

5. Roof light lower steelwork
139 × 10 mm CHS oval ring beam with welded cruciform section brackets at 1–1.8 m centres bolted to plate connector on primary ring beam.
Vapour barrier from roof lapped up and vulcanised to gasket at base of glazing.
50 mm insulation.
Curved mill finished aluminium flashing outside finish.

6. Glazing
100 × 50 mm white painted steel glazing bars.
8 mm toughened glass outer pane.
16 mm cavity with prismatic diffusers
12 mm laminated glass inner pane.

7. Maintenance access gantry
Galvanised steel grating spanning between galvanised steel flat brackets.
Handrail formed from 70 × 15 mm galvanised steel flats.

8. Roof light high level steelwork
139 × 10 mm CHS circular ring beam with three straight CHS cross members to support cone.
Mirror polished stainless steel sheet lining internally.

9. Cowl
3 mm aluminium plate curved over aluminium box section carcass.
Fixed bank of aluminium louvres rotating to face leeward side.
Cowl pivots around central point bearing at high level.
Rollers bearing on ring beam for guidance only.

10. Quadrant dampers
Circular soffit divided into four opening dampers supported on cruciform steel beams and controlled by building management system (BMS).

11. Reflector cone
2600 mm diameter cone with steel rectangular hollow section carcass and mirror polished stainless steel cladding.
Polyester powder coated waterproof aluminium evaporation tray for wind-blown water.
Steel tube welded to roof steel acts as guide for docking when cone is raised.
Mechanism for raising and lowering (not shown).

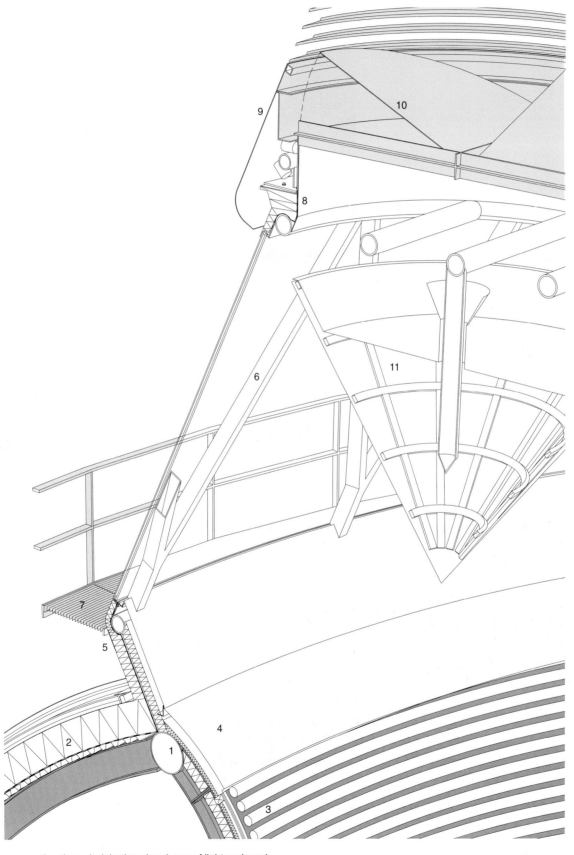

Cut-away section through debating chamber roof light and cowl

Photo credit: Charlotte Wood

Queens Road Community Centre, Walthamstow, London

Architect: Greenhill Jenner Architects
Services Engineer: Max Fordham LLP
Structural Engineer: Fluid Structures

The Community Centre provides a Sure Start nursery, a crèche, a lifelong learning and employment training centre for adults, meeting rooms and a multi-purpose hall in a socially deprived area of east London. The L-shaped plan encloses a veranda and 'play landscape', designed by Planet Earth Landscape Architects.

Pile foundations support a 300 mm thick concrete slab spanning made-up ground. A steel frame has been used for speed of construction with metal and timber stud infill to keep the weight down. Sustainable materials such as timber windows, Douglas fir rainscreen cladding and recyclable aluminium roofing have been used. The building makes good use of natural daylight and passive ventilation.

Photo credit: Charlotte Wood

The ground floor dayroom, crèche and daycare rooms facing the veranda are clad in Trespa, a flat panel based on thermosetting resins, homogeneously reinforced with wood fibres and manufactured under high pressure and at high temperatures.

To limit noise break-out from the multi-purpose hall to the surrounding residential area the acoustic performance of the envelope has been enhanced. The roof build-up incorporates a layer of dense acoustic insulation beneath the normal mineral wool insulation. In the walls a quilt made up from two layers of mineral wool with a 1.2 mm thick Xetal membrane has been hung between the metal studs. The membrane is made from recycled rubber with additives containing millions of nano-scale vacuums. A second layer of the membrane is sandwiched between the two layers of plasterboard lining. The variety of insulation ensures sound of different frequencies is absorbed.

Photo credit: Charlotte Wood

The architects have utilised a rich palette of materials to give the building life and freshness without resorting to simplistic gestures.

*Photo credit: Greenhill Jenner
Architects*

*Photo credit: Greenhill Jenner
Architects*

Site plan with area of detail shown in
red, scale 1:1000

1. Ground floor
75 mm fibre reinforced floor screed on 75 mm
expanded polystyrene insulation generally.
22 mm beech sprung floor on timber battens on
polypropylene cradles with 70 mm mineral wool
insulation in between to hall only.
Damp proof membrane.
300 mm thick reinforced concrete slab.
18 m deep concrete piles.
Minimum 50 mm sand blinding
Minimum 150 mm compacted hardcore.

2. External decking
145 × 32 mm untreated Iroko decking with anti-
slip grooves routed into surface.
150 × 50 mm tanalised softwood joists.

3. Structural frame
203 × 203 mm UC (universal column) section
steel columns in 2 storey hall wall.
150 × 150 mm SHS (square hollow section)
columns in single storey dayroom external wall.
254 × 254 mm UC section beam over doors to
veranda.
203 × 203 mm UC section main roof beams.

4. External wall to veranda
6 mm thick high-pressure-laminated rainscreen
cladding adhesive fixed to battens.
35 × 50 mm softwood battens forming 35 mm
ventilation gap.
Breather membrane.
9 mm plywood sheathing.
100 × 50 mm softwood studwork frame.
100 mm mineral wool between studs.
Vapour barrier fixed to inside of studs.
18 mm thick metal channel studs.
12.5 mm plasterboard.
13 mm high impact resistance plasterboard
internal lining with skim coat painted white.
100 × 18 mm painted MDF skirting.

5. Windows and doors
High performance soft-wood windows and
doors.
Douglas fir edge trims with clear varnish finish.

6. Ground floor roof
Mechanically fixed single-ply membrane.
85 mm rigid insulation.
Vapour control layer.
18 mm plywood deck with 1 degree fall made
up with softwood firrings.
9 mm plywood upstands at edges.
150 × 50 mm softwood joists.
70 × 38 mm softwood battens.

Two layers 12.5 mm plasterboard ceiling with
skim coat painted white.

7. Coping
Polyester powder coated aluminium coping.

8. Internal wall
13 mm high impact resistance plasterboard to
hall side with skim coat painted white.
1 mm acoustic membrane.
12.5 mm plasterboard.
94 mm thick metal studwork running full height
to roof of hall.
Acoustic insulation hung from metal studwork
made up from 2 layers 25 mm mineral wool quilt
with 1 mm acoustic membrane in between.
100 × 50 mm softwood studwork frame.
12.5 mm plasterboard.
13 mm high impact resistance plasterboard to
dayroom side with skim coat painted white.

9. Timber-clad external wall
96 × 19 mm horizontal Douglas Fir rainscreen
cladding boards with 15 mm open joints.
46 × 19 mm Douglas Fir boards every 6th
board.
25 × 38 mm vertical softwood battens creating
25 mm ventilation gap.
Breather membrane.
12 mm plywood sheathing.
100 × 50 mm softwood studwork.
Vapour barrier
94 mm thick metal studwork running full height
to roof of hall.
Acoustic insulation hung from metal studwork
made up of 2 layers 25 mm mineral wool quilt
with 1 mm acoustic membrane.
Two layers 12.5 mm plasterboard with 1 mm
acoustic membrane sandwiched in between
and taped to underside of metal roof deck.

10. Main roof
Aluminium standing seam roof sheets clipped
to support bar fixed through insulation to
structural decking on brackets at 1000 mm
centres.
180 mm mineral wool compressed to 150 mm.
Vapour control layer.
30 mm rigid slab acoustic insulation.
Galvanised steel structural deck spanning
between steels.
38 × 38 mm softwood battens.
Two layers 12.5 mm plasterboard with skim coat
painted white.

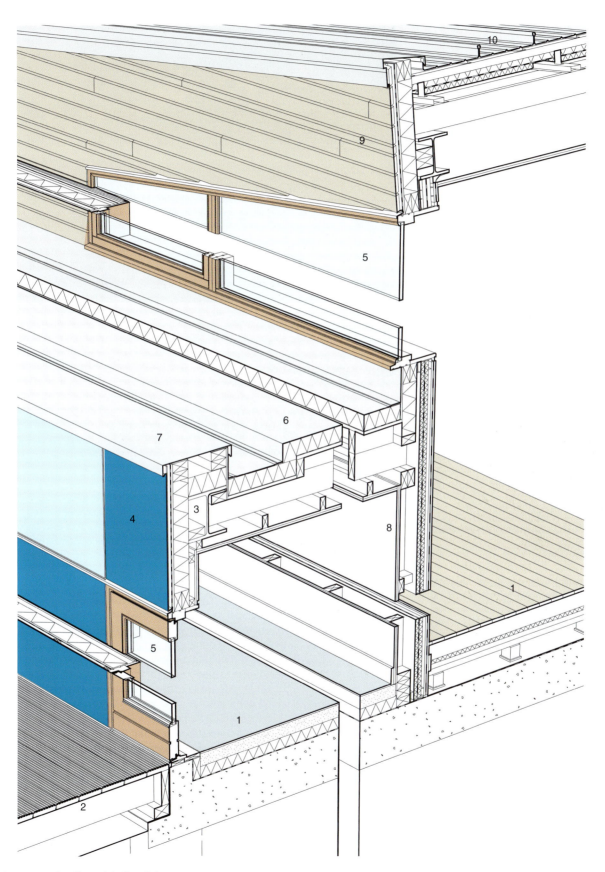

Cut-away section through hall and dayroom

Photo credit: National Maritime Museum

Sky Ear

Designer: Haque Design & Research
Electronics engineer: Senseinate Inc.
Structural engineer: Fluid Structures

Photo credit: David Rothschild

Sky Ear is a floating cloud of light that listens out for electromagnetic radiation in the air. A hovering structure made up of hundreds of helium filled balloons drifts through the evening skies. The cloud glows and flickers brightly as it passes through varying radio and microwave spaces generated by mobile phones, television broadcasts, wireless laptops and the electronic paraphernalia of modern life.

The structure is made up of 3.3 m diameter rings of carbon fibre tubing tied together in a hexagonal lattice. The largest flight yet, in Greenwich Park on 15 September 2004, consisted of 36 rings tethered to the ground at a height of 60–100 metres on three pairs of cables for stability. Clusters of 23–29 white latex balloons are packed tight into a fishing net bag stretched across each ring, with their round tops uppermost. The tops form a smooth convex upper surface while the underside, where the valves are, is uneven, causing a pressure differential which generates lift.

Each balloon contains a sensor circuit board taped to a vacuum formed neck plug and valve. The sensor detects electromagnetic radiation causing six ultra-bright coloured LEDs to illuminate. The sensors also communicate from one to the next via infrared transmitter/receivers. The range of each is only 30–50 cm so ripples of colour spread easily within a ring but not so easily from one ring to the next.

One balloon in each ring contains a mobile phone. During the performance the phone numbers were projected on to the ground for visitors to phone directly into the structure to create atmospheric disturbances inside the cloud and listen to the sounds of the sky.

Photo credit: David Rothschild

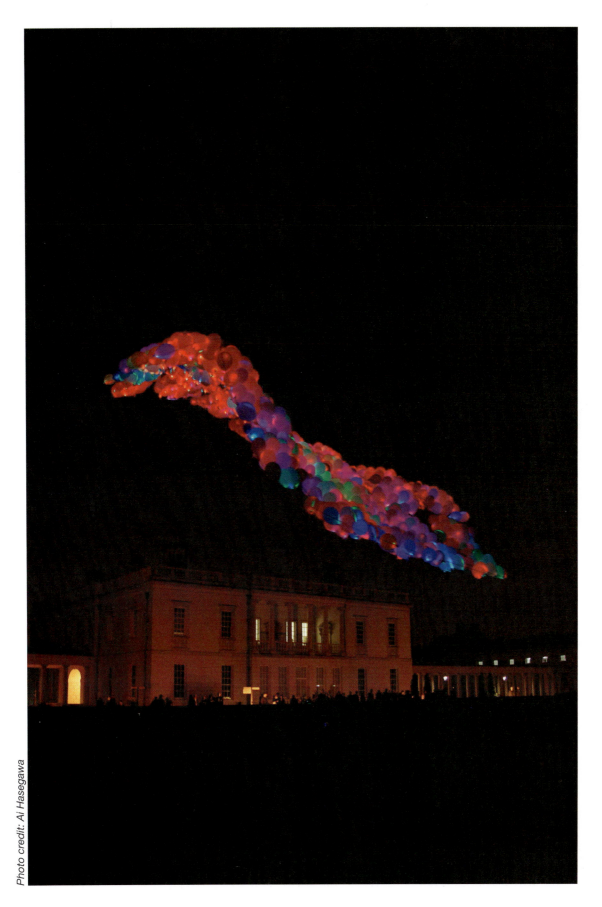

Photo credit: David Rothschild

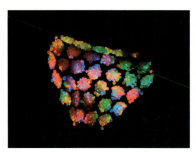

Photo credit: David Rothschild

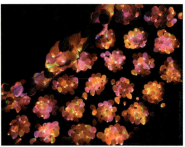

Photo credit: David Rothschild

1. Structural ring
8 mm diameter × 1.65 mm wall thickness carbon fibre rod.
Original 10 m length cut into four 2.5 m lengths for ease of transportation and rejoined using 200 mm length × 12.7 mm diameter carbon fibre sleeves to form 3.3 m diameter ring.
2.5 m lengths fit in an estate car and can be carried by air as skis.

2. Joints between rings
Adjacent rings overlapped and tied together with mountain climbing line in two locations to make the cloud structure more rigid and therefore more aerodynamic.
Experiments found that a single tie acted as a pin joint which easily twisted and snapped the carbon fibre.
Deformation of the cloud structure under various weather conditions was tested by hanging it upside down and loading it with weights in the same way Gaudi tested his roof structures.

3. Netting
Fishing net hand-sewn into bags to suit ring diameter.
Carbon fibre rods threaded through net to form ring.

4. Balloon
24 inch white latex balloons.
23–29 balloons packed into each net bag with valves facing down.
Each balloon provides approximately 100 g lift.

5. Neck plug
56 × 38 mm vacuum formed neck plug with valve for inflating balloon.
Plug is oval in plan to make fitting balloon easier.
Neck plug has a notch which the roll of the balloon mouth slips over and with which it engages.

6. Sensor
75 × 25 mm circuit board attached to neck plug with 1 inch fibreglass tape placed along entire back of sensor to protect balloon from damage from solder joints.
Eight ultra-bright LEDs per board connected to sensor.
Sensor is a simple gauss meter which measures magnetic induction.

7. Battery
Battery clipped to sensor board.

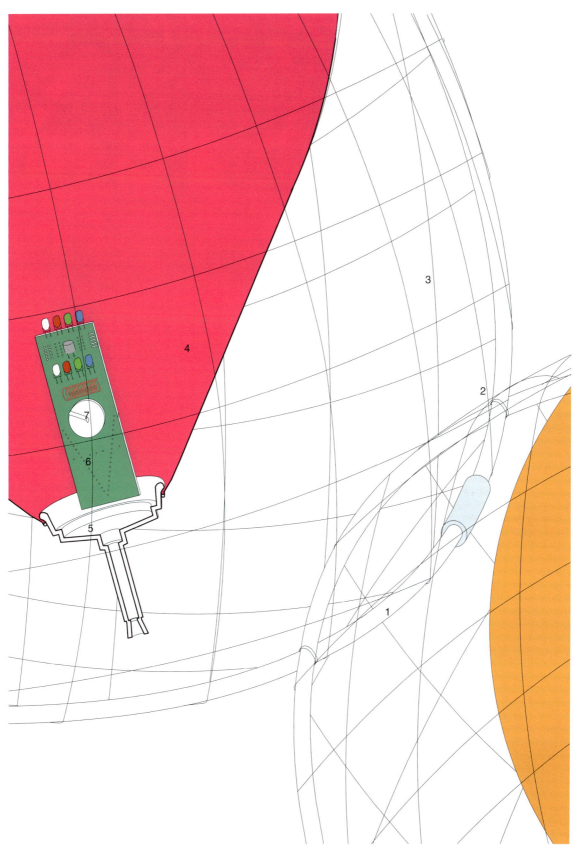

Cut-away section through edge of typical ring showing balloon valve and sensor circuit

Photo credit: Luke Lowings

Photo credit: Tim Soar / Tim Soar Photography

Salvation Army Chapel, London

Chapel Architect: Carpenter Lowings Architects
Building Architect: Sheppard Robson

The new headquarters of the Salvation Army lies on one of the most significant public routes in London, between the Millennium Bridge over the Thames and St Paul's Cathedral. Structural engineers Arup used post-tensioned slabs to reduce the depth of the floors, allowing a whole extra floor than what was originally envisaged within the height limits around St Paul's. In order to post-tension the slab, concrete steel rods are laid across the formwork, sheathed to prevent bonding to the concrete. Once the concrete has cured, the rods are tensioned, locked in position and the sheaths filled with grout.

Photo credit: Luke Lowings

At the west end, facing the pedestrian route, the office floors are lifted on raking white concrete H-frames creating a 'forum' space beneath containing a café and offices for the General and his staff above. The centrepiece is the chapel, which hangs at first floor over the entrance symbolising the spiritual calling at the centre of the Army's mission. At night it emits a fiery amber glow visible from a distance, its sloping face tilted towards the sky.

Inside, the chapel has an oak floor and a ceiling of oak veneered acoustic absorbent planks. The walls are a double skin construction to provide acoustic separation from the surrounding offices. Air is supplied through the cavity and is extracted through perforations in the ceiling to a plenum behind. The outer glass skin is acid etched while the inner skin has a gold coating which reflects sunlight or artificial lighting and fills the room with an orange glow. The acid-etched layer continues outside the building, wrapping around the roof and floor. Alternate panes of the inner layer pivot to allow cleaning of the cavity.

Photo credit: Graham Bizley

The furniture by Barber Osgerby is light and mobile so the chapel can be easily changed from a conventional format facing towards one end to a more informal meeting arrangement.

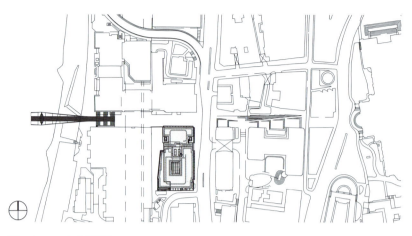

Site plan, scale 1:5000

Photo credit: Luke Lowings

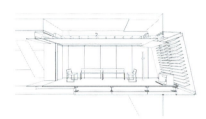

Perspective section

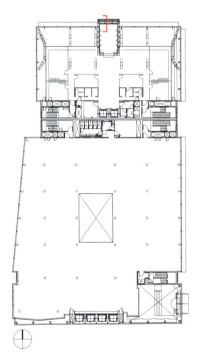

First floor plan, scale 1:850

The external 'sky wall' of the chapel tilts slightly and is made from clear glass. A bank of translucent and partially reflective blades obscures a direct view of the building opposite and reflects a view of the sky. The blades are angled differently so that they reflect a single image for a viewer at the door of the chapel. Clouds drift and the light changes over the course of the day, and through the seasons, making a peaceful other-worldly place for contemplation.

1. Steel structure
Two 150 × 100 mm RHS (rectangular hollow section) beams suspended from concrete second floor above.
150 × 90 mm rolled channel section and 150 × 100 mm RHS ties between RHS beams to support ceiling.
203 × 133 × 30 kg UB (universal beams) suspended from concrete second floor above to form chapel floor.
All steelwork to be intumescent painted white.

2. External building steelwork
406 × 178 mm × 74 kg UBs forming external framework supporting glass solar shading at second, third and fourth floors.

3. Sky wall structure
Four sided 120 × 120 mm SHS (square hollow section) frame with 120 × 25 mm channel welded to all sides all painted dark grey.
Two 100 × 50 mm RHS mullions welded to frame at glazing joints.
Sky wall frame fixed to main RHS beams with pin-joint connections.

4. Sky wall glazing
19.5 mm thick laminated glazing comprising 12 mm low-iron inner pane, 1.5 mm heat-rejecting interlayer and 6 mm low-iron outer pane.
Pressed stainless steel angle bonded to outer edges of façade glazing to protect interlayer.
Solid black frit border on inner face to cover steel frame behind with 30 mm gradation to clear.
Glass structurally bonded to fully welded frame of 50 × 25 × 6 mm polyester powder coated aluminium angles bolted to steel frame.

5. Louvre brackets
Two parallel 50 × 10 mm anodised aluminium flats clamped around mild steel lugs with spacers to form louvre support track.
12 mm thick laser cut profiled anodised aluminium flat bracket screwed to track spacer with two countersunk hex-head M6 25 mm stainless steel screws.
4 mm thick anodised aluminium plate bolted to bracket via slotted hole to allow tolerance and angle adjustment.
Bolts protruding from glass louvre fitted through bracket and secured with stainless steel dome head nuts.

6. Glass louvre
6 mm low-iron annealed float glass with colourless semi-reflective coating (on top surface).
0.76 mm PVB (polyvinylbutyral) sheet interlayer.
10 mm toughened glass acid-etched on lower surface.
All edges polished.
Four stainless steel bolts bonded into lower pane of glass using undercut glass anchors.

7. Acoustic timber ceiling
128 mm wide × 16 mm thick oak veneered MDF perforated tongued and grooved planks with fibreglass mat behind perforations.
15 mm shadow gap between inner glazing and edge of ceiling.
Fibreglass mat and insulation above ceiling down long sides of chapel.
Central area left clear to act as air extract plenum.

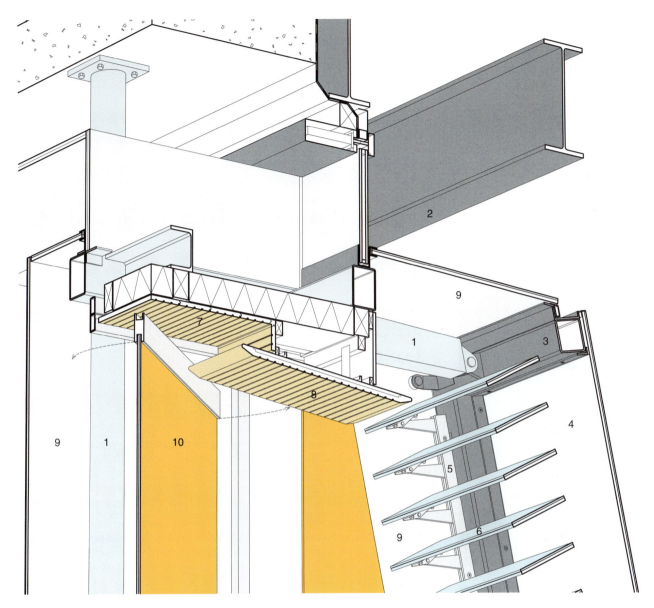

Cut-away section through top corner of external wall, ceiling and louvres

8. Acoustic timber baffle
740 mm wide baffle formed from 128 mm wide
× 16 mm thick oak veneered MDF perforated
tongued and grooved planks with 50 × 30 mm
profiled oak lips and fibreglass mat behind
perforations.
Baffle hung from softwood framework on
galvanised steel hangers.
12 mm thick painted MDF closer panel facing
window.

9. Outer leaf glazing
19.5 mm thick laminated glazing comprising
12 mm toughened low-iron inner pane, 1.5 mm
PVB interlayer and 6 mm toughened acid-
etched outer pane.
Inserts to be factory fitted to inner pane to
receive bolt fixings and covered by outer pane.

Void between inner and outer glazing acts as a
supply air plenum.

10. Inner leaf glazing (internal only)
2270 mm high × 1120 mm wide glazed
panels fixed up into two welded 60 × 30
× 3 mm RHS fixed via slotted holes to
100 × 100 × 8 mm equal angle bolted to
main steel SHS.
Alternate panels to open on central pivots to
allow cleaning inside cavity.
100 mm high proprietary door rail with satin
anodised aluminium cover plates.
13.5 mm orange/gold laminated glazing
comprising 6 mm coated annealed inner pane,
1.5 mm PVB interlayer and acid-etched outer
pane.

Photo credit: Tim Crocker

Photo credit: Whitby Bird

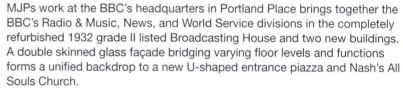

Photo credit: MacCormac Jamieson Pritchard Architects

Photo credit: Tim Crocker

BBC Broadcasting House, London

Architects: MacCormac Jamieson Prichard Architects
Structural and Façade Engineers: Whitbybird

MJPs work at the BBC's headquarters in Portland Place brings together the BBC's Radio & Music, News, and World Service divisions in the completely refurbished 1932 grade II listed Broadcasting House and two new buildings. A double skinned glass façade bridging varying floor levels and functions forms a unified backdrop to a new U-shaped entrance piazza and Nash's All Souls Church.

The design team wanted a calm uncluttered façade. To avoid too many movement joints the two seven-storey skins are hung independently from cantilevered brackets with a 1.2 m gap in between down which a cleaning cradle can pass, so there are no maintenance gantries. Very low wind speeds mean diagonal bracing can be eliminated by using rigid connections.

The inner skin hangers, restrained laterally by the floor slabs, are custom-made steel sections with steel angle transoms. Drained aluminium glazing channels are fixed to the steel frame and double-glazed units are fixed to the channels with structural silicone. Portland stone panels conceal the depth of the floors and provide some privacy for workers inside.

The heat load of the building is very high from lighting and electrical equipment so the outer skin provides crucial solar shading. The outer pane of the single laminated glass sheets has an acid-etched pattern and the inner pane has a fritted pattern, which overlay to give a matt tone similar to Portland stone. The glass is bolted to shot-peened stainless steel brackets bolted to the hangers via rigid moment connections. The outer skin hangers are propped back to the inner skin with stainless steel struts that can move in the vertical direction but are rigid in the horizontal direction. To transfer the wind load through the inner glazing the struts are fixed to a continuous angle bolted through the glazing joints to the transoms behind.

In certain locations small balconies cantilever out from the floors. The fronts of the balconies are Portland stone-faced pre-cast concrete units which sit flush with the outer skin glazing allowing more direct views out.

Photo credit: Tim Crocker

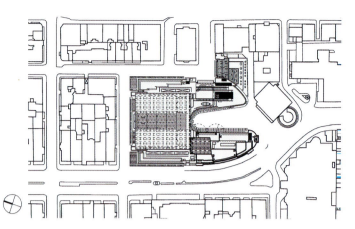

Site plan, scale 1:3000

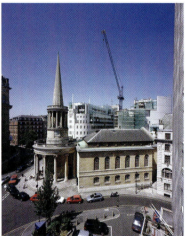

Photo credit: Tim Crocker

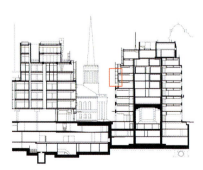

East – west section, scale 1:1500

1. Main building structure
Primary steel structure with reinforced concrete floor slabs.

2. Internal skin structure
Painted steel hangers at nominal 2200 mm centres made up from 100 × 100 mm SHS (square hollow section) welded to interrupted 100 × 20 mm deep web welded to 100 × 20 mm front flange.
100 × 100 × 20 mm painted steel angle transoms with countersunk bolt connections to mullions.

3. Internal skin glazing
70 × 34 mm anodised aluminium sub-frame with drainage fixed to steel transoms and mullions.
Double-glazed units fixed to aluminium sub-frame with horizontal pressure plates and hidden toggle fixings to vertical mullions.
8 mm clear outer pane with solar coating to inner face, 16 mm cavity, 13.5 mm laminated inner pane.

4. Internal skin solid panel
100 mm thick insulated aluminium sandwich panel fixed on brackets to steel mullions and transoms.
50 mm Portland stone facing panel fixed with hidden undercut anchor fixings to sandwich panel.

5. External skin structure
75 × 40 mm stainless steel hanger with bead-blasted finish.
Stainless steel crossbar brackets bolted to hanger.

6. Wind load restraint
75 × 40 mm stainless steel wind strut with bead-blasted finish bolted to hanger with rigid moment connection for horizontal/lateral loads and a pin-jointed connection to allow unrestrained vertical movements of the external skin structure.
70 × 60 mm stainless steel angle with bead-blasted finish fixed through inner skin glazing joints as pressure plate capping with welded flat bracket for connection of wind strut to inner skin steel transoms.

7. External skin clear glazing
Laminated glass bolted to crossbar brackets via stainless steel spacers.
10 mm clear low-iron outer pane and 8 mm clear inner pane.

8. External skin fritted glazing
Laminated glass bolted to crossbar brackets via stainless steel spacers.
10 mm low-iron outer pane with acid-etched rectangle pattern to break up reflections and 8 mm inner pane with white fritted square pattern.

9. Balcony floor
Raised floor system on adjustable pedestals.
203 × 203 mm × 60 kg UC (universal column) beams cantilevered from main building structure.
130 mm thick reinforced concrete slab cast into webs of steel beams.
100 mm insulation.
Polyester powder coated pressed metal ceiling panel.

10. Balcony external wall
60 × 60 × 6 mm SHS (square hollow section) vertical steel frame bolted to UC edge beam.
130 mm pre-cast concrete façade panel with 75 mm Portland stone facing clamped to steel frame with 45 mm ventilation gap behind.
Polyester powder coated aluminium sheet fixed to both sides of vertical steel frame with thermal insulation in between.
150 mm wide pressed stainless steel edge trim channel to all four sides of pre-cast panel.

11. Balcony internal glazing
Full height double-glazed side panels fixed to steel at bottom.
Front and roof panels bolted to side panels via countersunk stainless steel connectors.
All double-glazed sealed units have 10 mm clear outer pane with solar coating to inner face, 10 mm cavity, 16.5 mm laminated inner pane.

12. Balcony gutter
Special powder coated steel transom with 410 × 20 mm steel plate welded to bottom leg.
Aluminium gutter on rigid insulation with trace heating and spout to direct water away from building face.
Stainless steel flashing to glazing above.

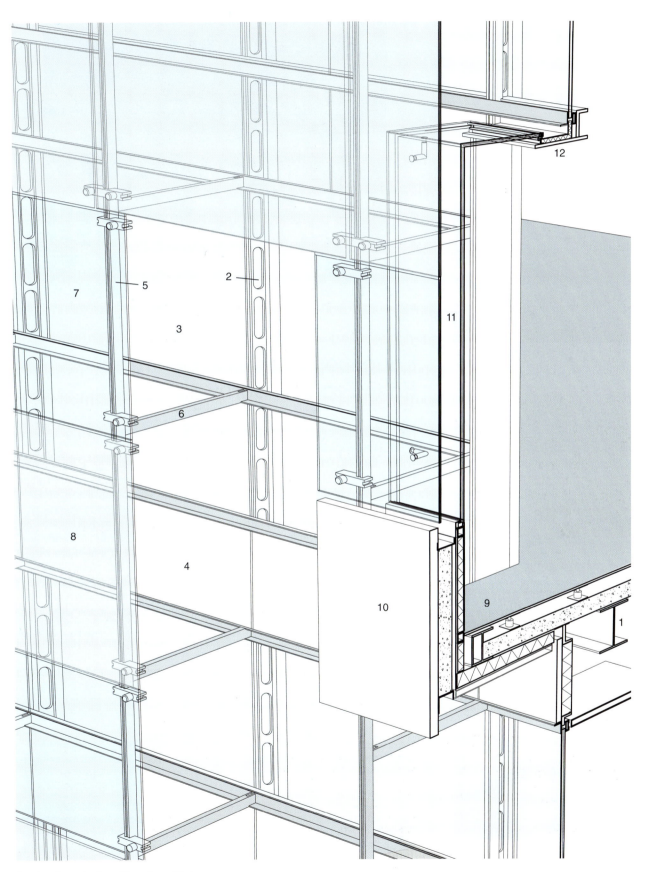

Section through glazed façade and balcony

Photo credit: Adam Parker

Photo credit: Grimshaw

Photo credit: Adam Parker

Photo credit: Adam Parker

Education Resource Centre
Eden Project, Cornwall

Architect: Nicholas Grimshaw & Partners
Structural Engineers: SKM Anthony Hunts

The Education Resource Centre contains children's classrooms, an exhibition space and a café to fulfil the Eden Project's aim of educating visitors about the importance of plants within our ecosystem. Sited next to the Humid Tropics and Warm Temperate Biomes, the Centre's form is derived from phyllotaxis, the mathematical process that determines the form of nearly all plant growth including such patterns as the arrangement of leaves around a stem or scales on a pinecone. Rapid prototyping was used to develop the building's structure using data from Grimshaw's three-dimensional CAD model. The data was translated directly to a physical model of the roof structure by selective laser sintering – a process by which a laser beam solidifies a polymer powder into a thermoplastic solid.

The roof structure is a grid of laminated spruce beams spanning from a central steel ring beam to three concrete buttress 'feet' at the perimeter. Each beam spans two bays between the mid-points of two other beams fixed with steel plate connectors. The actual components were fabricated directly from a computer model based on SKM Anthony Hunts' structural calculations. Each beam was individually formed with a curve in two directions. Further machining of the faces was then done by a computer-controlled 5-axis CNC (computer numerically controlled) cutter capable of drilling, cutting, planing or trimming the timber.

The roof geometry is like a sweep of repetitive radial segments that vary in length. Each segment is the same and has been prefabricated as a set of timber elements. Timber roof panels have been prefabricated in a series of graduated sizes to fit the double-curved radiating segments of the lattice – the only way a repetitive module can be formed to fit the roof profile. School groups frequently use the building so control of noise is important. The ceiling is the exposed

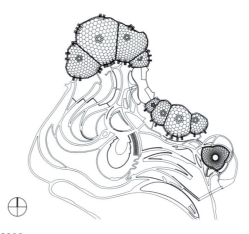

Site plan, scale 1:8000

plywood on the underside of the panels, punctured with holes to absorb sound. Protruding pyramids with operable windows provide ventilation and illumination to the exhibition space and café below. The panels are clad with standing seam copper panels replicating the pattern of scales on a pinecone.

Photo credit: Nicholas Grimshaw & Partners

Model of timber roof structure

1. Roof structure
Spruce glue-lam roof beams nominally 820 mm high × 220 mm wide joined to form grid-shell structure.
Each beam spans two bays; lengths vary from 3–12 m.
Each beam fabricated with a curve in both directions, then faces cut individually on 5-axis cutter with different curvature.

2. Beam connection bracket
650 × 180 mm galvanised steel brackets bolted through timber beams at mid-span with connecting plates to receive beam end plates.

3. Beam end plate
Two 660 × 310 mm galvanised steel flitch plates fixed into slots in ends of timber beams with fifty-four 10 mm galvanised steel dowels.
Beams bolted on to connection brackets with three 24 mm galvanised steel dowels.

4. Prefabricated acoustic roof panels
Prefabricated spiral roof panels incorporating vapour barrier, insulation and breather membrane (items 5–8).
15 mm birch plywood soffit with 16 mm diameter perforations at 32 mm centres to allow sound penetration to insulation behind.
200 × 157 mm service void running axially along the length of each panel.
22 mm OSB (orientated strand board) upstands cut to profile to form fall for OSB decking.
Nominal 200 × 50 mm vent slots cut in plywood upstands to allow ventilation behind OSB deck.

5. Vapour barrier

6. Insulation
313 mm thick recycled cellulose insulation blown in to cavity in timber panel as thermal insulation and acoustic absorbent.

7. Plywood tray
15 mm plywood fixed on battens over insulation.

8. Breather membrane
Breather membrane fixed over plywood carcass with ventilation void above.

9. Spiral gutter
Mechanically fixed EPDM gutter falling to perimeter gutters at centre and leading edges of roof.
Breather membrane between EPDM and insulation.

10. Roof deck
22 mm OSB decking in triangular segments fixed down to OSB upstands to minimum 1:60 fall.

11. Isolating layer
Rubberised asphalt lining membrane.

12. Copper cladding
0.7 mm gauge long seam copper roofing in 600 mm widths fixed to OSB deck with copper clips.
Initial colour to be natural copper which will dull to brown and gradually develop a green patina.

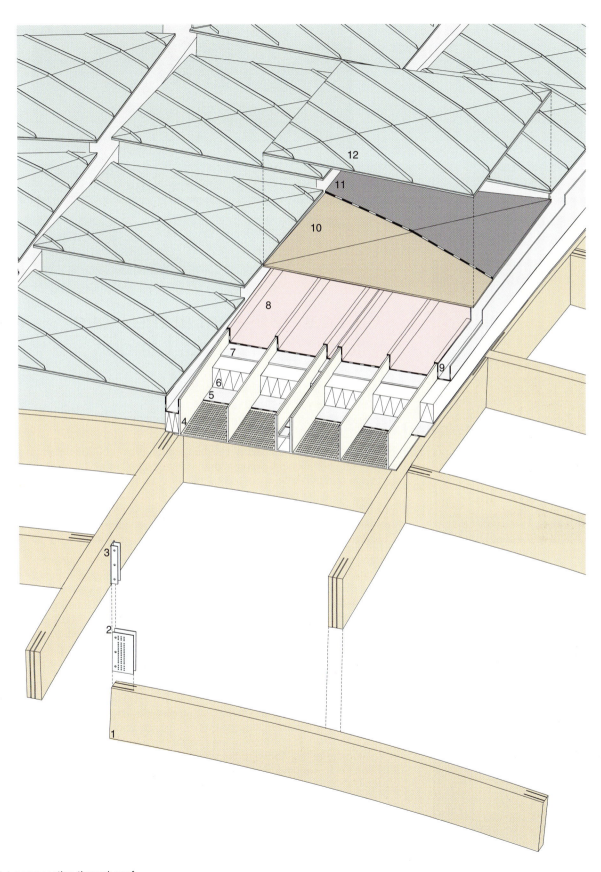

Cut-away section through roof

Photo credit: Morley von Sternberg

Hunterian Museum at the Royal College of Surgeons, London

Architects: Julian Bicknell & Associates
Exhibition Design: John Ronayne
Specialist Subcontractor: Netherfield Visual Ltd

The Royal College of Surgeons' museum contains over 3000 anatomical specimens, pathological preparations, natural history exhibits, fossils, paintings and drawings collected by John Hunter (1728–1793). At its centre the Crystal Gallery occupies an 8 m high room in a part of the college rebuilt in the 1950s after wartime damage. Air conditioning and lighting have been seamlessly integrated with three levels of bespoke display cabinets to make a two-storey glass-lined room.

A fibrous plaster suspended ceiling has been installed in three vaulted sections similar to that in the original 1815 building by George Dance. Supply air ducts descend in the four corners distributing air through grilles in the base of the cabinets at ground and first floor levels. Concealed fibre optic heads are mounted within the shelf edges, with cables back to projectors at either end of each cabinet. The projectors sit on steel mesh shelves contained in a steel casing. Extract air can be drawn up past them, dissipating heat, to the ceiling void and out via plant on the roof.

Photo credit: Morley von Sternberg

The lower display cabinets sit on a plinth on the ground floor. The central and upper cabinets sit on C shaped brackets fixed to the existing first floor slab edge which has been strengthened with a new steel beam to take the extra load of all the glass. Each laminated sheet weighs about 30 kg. There is a 20 mm movement joint between the central and lower cabinets to allow for deflection of the first floor and the upper cabinets are restrained back to the roof soffit with a sliding connection that allows vertical movement.

The bespoke cabinets are made up of standard components assembled to suit the specific space. A primary steel structure supports secondary aluminium members which carry the glass doors. The 10.8 mm laminated glass does not require side frames, enabling cabinets to be joined together to make a seamless glass enclosure.

Surrounding the visitor with glass jars is a theatrical gesture, intended to put you inside John Hunter's mind and understand how he saw his own work.

Photo credit: Morley von Sternberg

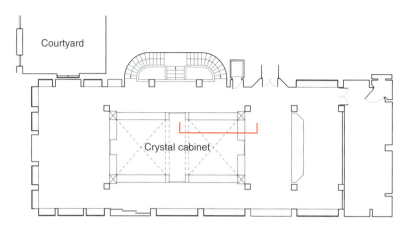

Upper floor plan, scale 1:300

Photo credit: Morley von Sternberg

1. Existing building structure
Existing 500 × 500 mm concrete columns in each corner.

2. First floor
Existing concrete slab with downstand edge.
New steel beam to strengthen floor edge to carry eccentric loading from cabinets.
New hardwood flooring on softwood battens.

3. Ceiling
Domed suspended ceiling made from prefabricated fibrous plaster segments fixed to galvanised steel support rails suspended from roof.

4. Cabinet support brackets
Steel C-brackets at 800 mm centres formed from two lengths of 120 × 80 mm RHS (rectangular hollow section) welded to 120 × 25 mm plate bolted to first floor slab to support middle and upper cabinets.
Steel brackets at 800 mm centres formed from cranked 120 × 80 mm RHS fixed to roof soffit to provide head restraint for upper cabinets.

5. Plinth
18 mm plywood base laid on floor over footprint of cabinet.
30 × 30 mm SHS (square hollow section) steel plinth structure.
50 × 50 × 3 mm steel angles welded to legs of plinth with four 50 mm diameter adjustable feet per bay.

6. Shelf supports
Pair of 76 × 38 mm RHS steel tubes with 4 mm gap between.
4 mm thick mild steel shelf brackets bolted between RHS posts.
Folded 2 mm steel cross members bolted between posts to form central supports for glass shelves.

7. Shelves
2 mm folded mild steel shelf edge spanning between shelf support brackets to support front edge of glass shelves and to house fibre optic heads.
80 mm wide folded steel label rail screwed to shelf edge. Angle of label rail varies depending on height of shelf.

10.8 mm clear laminated glass shelves on foam strips.

8. Fibre optic lighting
Fibre optic light source projectors on shelves made from 50 × 50 mm steel mesh mounted in sheet steel duct cupboard to allow hot air to rise to ceiling void above.
Fibre optic cables concealed in shelf edge profiles with heads at 100 mm centres.

9. Air conditioning
740 × 700 mm service zone in corner between cabinets.
500 × 400 mm air supply duct feeding to 300 × 100 mm ducts connected to grilles in plinths at low level on ground and first floors.
Air extracted with roof level fans to ceiling void through void in service zone around supply duct and through fibre optic lighting cupboards.

10. Cabinet frames
Extruded aluminium box-sections bolted together at corners with angle plates and bolted to steel to form frames at top and bottom of each cabinet. Extrusions have channels to accept sliding gear, hinges and locks for cabinet doors.

11. Cabinet doors
125 × 25 mm extruded aluminium frames top and bottom on sliding runners or hinged off cabinet frame.
Single fixed pane at first floor high level on void side.
10.8 mm clear laminated glass generally with frameless sides.
12 mm clear toughened glass at first floor on floor side to provide barrier loading.

12. Skirting
18 mm zero formaldehyde MDF plinth panel and skirting painted black.
Black extruded aluminium ventilation grille running full length at ground and first floor levels.

13. Movement joint
20 mm horizontal movement joint between lower and middle cabinets to allow for deflection of floor.

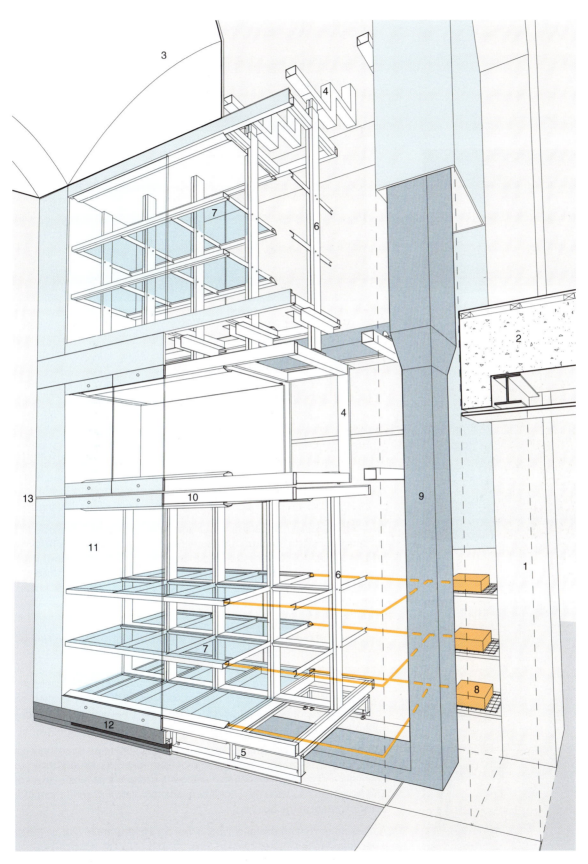

Cut-away section through Crystal Cabinet

Photo credit: Rogier van der Heide / Arup

Photo credit: Christian Richters

Photo credit: Rogier van der Heide / Arup

Photo credit: Rogier van der Heide / Arup

Galleria Fashion Mall, Seoul, South Korea

Architect: UN studio
Lighting Design: Rogier van der Heide, Arup Lighting

The Galleria was a dull shopping centre in Seoul with blind concrete walls. UN Studio and Arup Lighting have transformed it into a glowing light box with patterns of colour moving around the façades and messages flashing across it.

Two of the original concrete façades facing the street have been clad in a shimmering curtain of 850 mm diameter acid-etched glass discs held in a steel framework. The discs are suspended in threes on a steel strut that is suspended off a lattice of diagonal box-section members. The lattice is held off the existing concrete walls on brackets connected to I-section posts bolted to the walls.

Each of the 4340 discs has its own individually controlled luminaire. An innovative LED system was developed with Xilver Lighting of The Netherlands that can render 16 million different colours of light from just four LEDs. When creating white and pastel shades LEDs tend to drift towards a pink and magenta hue so there are two green LEDs, a red and a blue in each set. Contrary to popular belief LEDs can get very hot so they are mounted on a circular aluminium block that acts as a heat sink. The luminaires project the light off-centre on the glass discs to create an illusion that they are spherical.

A control box mounted on the diagonal lattice is shared by three luminaires. The control system, supplied by E:cue of Germany, runs 15 000 DMX channels and is arguably the most elaborate system of its kind in the world. The designers can write new configurations remotely and send them to a control system in the building.

According to lighting designer Rogier van der Heide people stop in the street, video it and take pictures of each other in front of it. The hackers of Seoul must be hard at work in their bedrooms working out how to take it over and broadcast their own messages.

Photo credit: Christian Richters

Photo credit: Rogier van der Heide / Arup

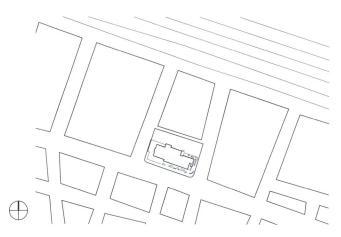

Site plan, scale 1:3000

1. Glass discs
850 mm diameter laminated glass disc made from two 6 mm toughened glass pieces with dichroic film interlayer to give the building a pearlescent effect during the day.
Disc frosted on rear face to diffuse light and frosted on front face to reduce glare to passing motorists.

2. Glazing support struts
50 mm high triangular steel strut with three steel glazing clamps.
Glazing clamped to strut with rubber gaskets in three places to minimise vibration.

3. Support bar
1700 mm long 50 × 50 × 4 mm steel SHS (square hollow section) support bar.

4. Luminaires
75 mm diameter circular cast aluminium heat sink mounting block bolted to support bar on steel brackets.
Two green, one blue, one red LED per lumin-aire glued to metal cored circuit board with thermally conductive glue to transmit heat to mounting block.
Hemi-spherical polycarbonate cover rated IP68 against water penetration.

5. Support brackets
One pair of 50 × 50 × 4 mm support brackets for each support bar bolted to lattice frame.

6. Lattice frame
Lattice framework of 120 × 50 × 5 mm SHS steel sections suspended off diagonal struts.

7. Diagonal struts
60 × 60 × 3.2 mm SHS diagonal steel struts to support lattice.

8. Primary structural supports
Steel support brackets bolted into existing concrete wall.
150 × 170 mm I-sections fixed with steel angle cleats to support brackets.

9. Original wall
Reinforced concrete wall of original building.

10. Control equipment
One control box mounted on diagonal lattice per three luminaires.
Each LED has been visually tested for colour variance against a control sample. The control box adjusts the colour curve specifically for that LED.

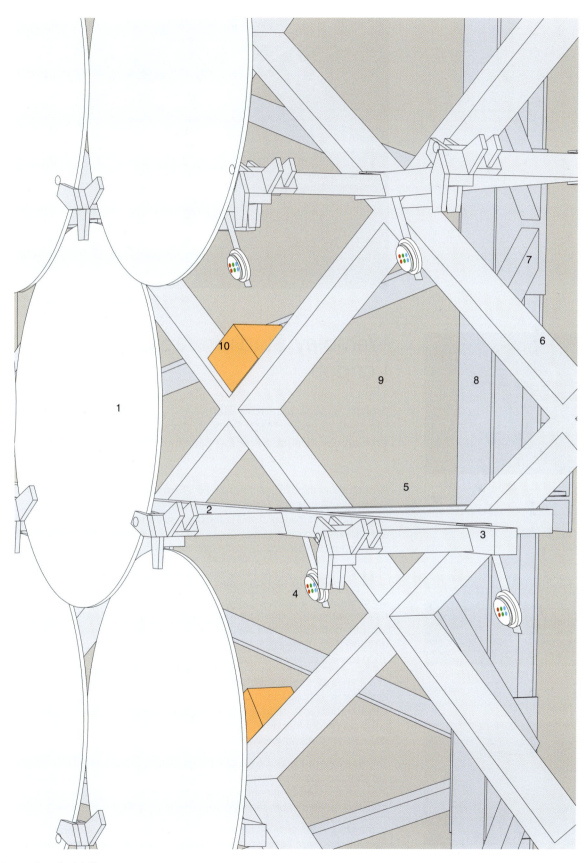

Cut-away façade detail

Wembley Stadium Arch, London

Architects: World Stadium Team
Structural Engineer: Mott Stadium Consortium
Arch steelwork subcontractor: Cleveland Bridge

An arch spanning 315 m across the new Wembley Stadium is a landmark visible across London. The 90 000-seat stadium boasts the biggest single-span roof structure in the world and is the biggest stadium with covered seating anywhere. The challenge was to provide a column free interior to the stadium, but without structure above that might impede operation of the retractable roof.

The arch was built in segments flat on the ground and hoisted up to an angle of 22°. On one side eight sets of 150 mm diameter stainless steel cables are strung from it to support the north roof's leading edge while backstay cables on the other side tie it to the seating bowl. It also provides 60% of the support for the south roof via underslung trusses – two running horizontally on either side of the stadium. The roof area is 4.5 hectares, with a weight of 7000 tonnes, of which 1.5 hectares is moveable.

The arch is a 7 m diameter 'basket weave' structure made from 457 mm diameter steel hollow sections with a series of steel rings at 9 m centres. At either end the arch narrows to a 1.5 m diameter 'pencil end' where the tubes are brought together on to a bearing. The steelwork was welded together on site over a 10-month period.

The bearings at the two ends work in two ways. During erection a temporary pin joint allowed the arch to rotate. This pin was then permanently welded in place and the permanent bearing is a simple ball and socket joint held in place by the force from the arch.

In the ground the arch is carried on 19 concrete piles connected by a 20 m diameter pile cap. There are ten metres of made-up ground and the site boundary is very close so a cylindrical concrete structure transfers the load down the axis of the arch to the centre of the pile cap.

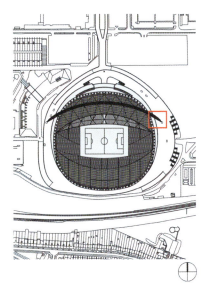

Site plan, scale 1:10000

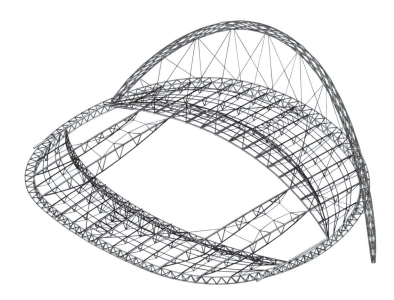

Axonometric showing arch and roof structure only

Photo credit: Foster + Partners

A cast steel drum transfers the load from the steel structure into the concrete. Because the bearings are such crucial elements of the design – any failure would be catastrophic – the engineers had to provide a 'robust' solution with alternative load paths. Although the bearing surface of the drum's top plate on the concrete is sufficient to carry the load on its own the drum is penetrated by reinforcement rods cast into the concrete that can also carry the entire load in shear.

Once the arch was fully loaded the steel bearings were encased in concrete. Maintenance can be carried out from a cart that can be driven through the centre of the arch structure.

Photo credit: Foster + Partners

1. Steel arch truss
Steel arch truss made up from 45 segments.
All truss members are 457 mm diameter steel CHSs (circular hollow sections) with wall thickness varying from 15 to 60 mm depending on local loads.
7.5 m diameter steel rings at 10 m centres with welded triangular bracing made up from RHSs (rectangular hollow sections).
1 m lengths of tube were factory-welded to circular rings.
8 m straight lengths of tube were site-welded to join the prefabricated ring pieces.

2. Pencil end
The last four segments of the truss taper down to a 1500 mm diameter at the end.
Ends of tubes are machined and welded to a 2 m diameter end plate.

3. Thrust bearing
800 mm diameter × 500 mm thick steel pin with curved lower surface machined to fit into dished top plate of rotation bearing.
300 mm diameter hole in centre of bearing for power and communications cables for lighting in arch.

4. Rotation bearing
Pin-joint bearing welded up from steel plates and bolted down to steel insert in concrete base.

300 mm diameter steel pin for rotating arch from ground to upright position.
Steel pin welded in place once arch fully loaded.

5. Steel insert
2.6 m diameter × 3 m deep × 70 mm thick steel tube insert cast into concrete base.
300 mm thick steel plate welded to top of insert to sit on concrete base.
Threaded bolts welded to plate to locate rotation bearing.
Reinforcement bars penetrating through holes in tube and cast into concrete as alternative load path.

6. Concrete pile cap
500 mm thick reinforced concrete top slab supported on beams and four 500 mm square concrete columns below.
6500 mm high × 500 mm thick reinforced concrete base ring to spread load through fill layer to pile cap.
2750 mm thick reinforced concrete pile cap.
Nineteen 1500 mm diameter concrete piles supporting pile cap.

7. Cone casing
Concrete base casing cast in-situ around bearing once rotation bearing welded in permanent position.

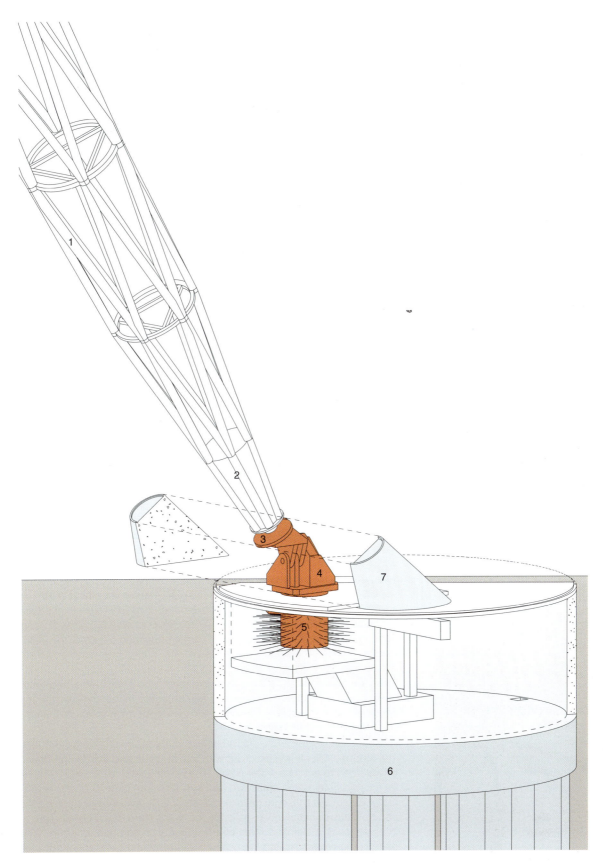

Cut-away section of arch showing base plinth connection and substructure

Photo credit: Kim Wilkie

Photo credit: Kim Wilkie

Photo credit: Kim Wilkie

Victoria & Albert Museum Courtyard, London

Landscape Architect: Kim Wilkie Associates
Lighting Design: Patrick Woodroffe

The new garden at the centre of the Victoria & Albert Museum combines the traditional simplicity of a garden courtyard with the drama and flexibility of a stage set. A paved ellipse creates a calm centre to the garden surrounded by lawns, lemon trees in glass planters and two larger liquidambar trees. The 70 × 40 m courtyard has always been an oasis amongst the labyrinthine galleries of the V&A but, prior to the renovation, grass mounds and Italian alder and cyprus trees made it rather claustrophobic.

Twenty-two etched glass tree planters mark the path around the perimeter of the lawns. The trees will be contained in glass reinforced plastic (GRP) liners so they can be easily lifted in and out. A decorative GRP sleeve inserted between the liner and the glass has a grey finish to give the glass an even appearance. Strips of LEDs are fixed to the underside edges of the glass planters making the sides glow white.

The York stone pieces that make up the steps and ramps have been cut individually using digitally-controlled equipment to fit the complex geometry. Strips of LEDs in plastic tubes concealed beneath the nosings of the treads wash the step below with light.

The stepped ellipse is picked out with jets of water and the central drain can be reversed to act as a water outlet. The holding tank for the fountains had to be located outside the courtyard and two 132 mm diameter ducts were laid under one of the museum galleries to reach it. To avoid any soil disturbance and possible damage in the galleries the ducts were thrust bored. This involves using a stainless steel tube with teeth on one end as a core drill. The earth is then removed and the core drill becomes the permanent duct. The central space can be flooded with water from the tank to create a shallow reflecting pool, or filled with heavy fog for night lighting.

Photo credit: Kim Wilkie

Photo credit: Kim Wilkie

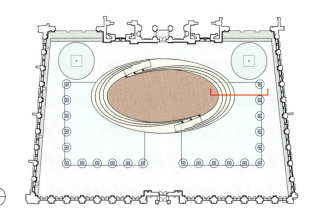

Site plan, scale 1:1000

1. Stone steps
125 mm thick Crosland Hill York stone step.
Dense concrete blockwork built up as
necessary to build up levels of steps and
ramps.
Each stone forming steps cut to unique shape
using computer-controlled cutting equipment.
Protruding nosing conceals half-round groove
in underside to house LED lighting.
Extruded plastic sleeve with sealed LEDs fixed
into drip groove to wash step below with light.

2. Ellipse stone paving
50 mm thick dark red Chinese sandstone
bedded on 75 mm sand–cement mortar.
Mastic asphalt tanking to ellipse slab and
retaining walls.

3. Ellipse concrete slab
150 mm thick fibre-reinforced concrete slab.
50 mm sand blinding.
150 mm hardcore.

4. Planter foundation
150 mm thick mass concrete foundation with
central cable duct for power cables.
50 mm sand blinding.
150 mm hardcore.

5. Planter base
1000 × 1000 × 100 mm thick Crosland Hill
York stone slab with central hole pre-drilled for
power cables.

6. Planter plinth
Galvanised steel plinth made from welded
100 × 75 mm steel RHSs (rectangular hollow
sections).
Cut-outs left in steel for lifting by fork-lift truck.

7. Planter glass casing
1000 × 1000 × 925 mm planter case made
from 25 mm thick sheets of toughened glass
mitred and silicone jointed at corners.
Glass acid etched on outer faces.

Thirty-six 50 mm diameter holes drilled in glass
base at 100 mm centres for drainage.
Base bolted to steel plinth below through glass
bottom of casing with rubber isolation washers
to prevent damage to glass.

8. Inner plant container
784 × 784 × 710 mm high liner made from GRP
(glass reinforced plastic) sheet.
20 mm return on all sides at top of liner for
stiffness.
Drainage holes in bottom of liner.
Geotextile membrane lining to planter to allow
water to drain without loss of soil.

9. Decorative sleeve
720 mm high GRP sheet decorative sleeve
with matt grey external finish between plant
container and glass.
200 mm wide GRP sheet top plate attached
to sleeve to cover gap between liner and
glass case.

10. Planter top
Geotextile membrane.
Four spotlights in corners of planter lid to light
trees from below.
15–20 mm diameter recycled glass pebbles.

11. Tree
Twenty-two trees brought to site in plant
containers and changed twice annually.
Lemon tree (Citrus lemon) during summer
months.
Holly tree (Ilex aquifolium) during winter months.

12. Duct
Service duct around perimeter of lawn carrying
electrical cables for lighting.
500 mm wide concrete lid with Crosland Hill
York stone capping.
Concrete slab floor with brickwork walls.

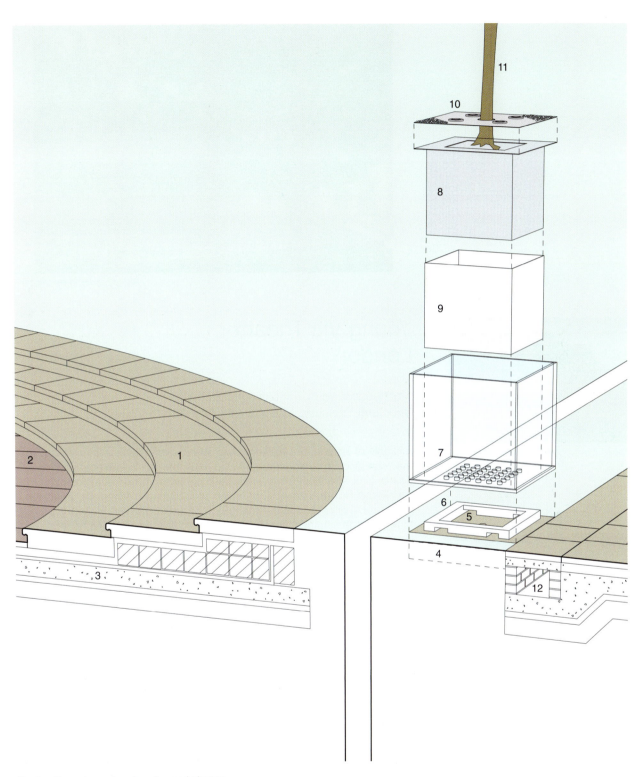

Section through courtyard paving and planter

Photo credit: Philip Vile

Young Vic Theatre, London

Architect: Haworth Tompkins Architects
Structural Engineer: Jane Wernick Associates

A jumble of old and new elements has been woven together to revitalise the Young Vic, an independent-minded experimental theatre near London's South Bank. The theatre's previous building dates from 1970 and despite its exposed concrete blockwork walls and simple bench seating, the audience has a strong affection for its informality. The architects have worked hard to preserve the atmosphere and new architectural interventions have been carefully balanced with continuity.

A converted Victorian terraced house known as the 'butcher's shop' forms the entrance into a new double height foyer with a studio theatre and back of house facilities beyond. The raft foundation, ground floor walls and first floor balconies of the existing auditorium have been retained and a new steel framed structure built around them to support a new roof, façade and lighting gantries.

Additional loading of the raft is not possible so the steel frame is supported independently on piled foundations around it. Only on the west side does the roof structure bear directly on the columns. On the north and south sides the building has been pushed right out to the pavement so there is no room for columns except in the corners. On the east side the columns have to sidestep the scene dock doors. Giant trusses on these three sides transfer the roof load to the columns. Two primary walk-through double trusses span east to west and a lattice of smaller walkways is suspended between them for hanging lighting.

The new steel frame uses the existing blockwork walls for wind bracing. Two new concrete ring beams in the blockwork are bolted to the steel frame via brackets with slotted holes and neoprene washers to prevent any vertical load transfer. New walkways hung from the roof outside the existing walls transfer windloads to the edges of the auditorium and into the ring beams.

The steel frame enables circulation, acoustics, thermal performance and technical facilities to be vastly improved whilst maintaining the intimate atmosphere of the much-loved auditorium.

Photo credit: Philip Vile

Photo credit: Philip Vile

Photo credit: Philip Vile

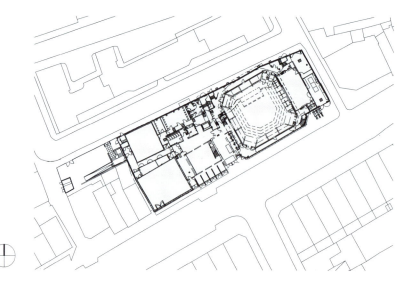

Site plan, scale 1:1500

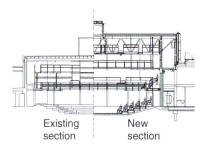

Existing section | New section

Section showing old and new construction, scale 1:500

Photo credit: Haworth Tompkins

1. Existing raft
Existing concrete raft under main auditorium retained.
Edge of slab made good for application of waterproof membrane.
Raft edge underpinned along north edge.

2. New foundations
Concrete piles with reinforced concrete pile caps to transfer load from steel columns to piles.

3. Steel columns
Two primary steel UC (universal column) columns on each elevation.

4. South side perimeter truss
2600 mm deep steel truss spanning between primary columns.
457 × 191 mm × 67 kg UB (universal beam) top chord.
356 × 171 mm × 51 kg UB bottom chord.
152 × 152 mm × 30 kg UC vertical members.
178 × 102 mm × 19 kg UB diagonal members.

5. East side perimeter truss
2600 mm deep steel truss spanning between primary columns.
406 × 178 mm × 60 kg UB top chord.
406 × 178 mm × 54 kg UB bottom chord.
152 × 152 mm × 37 kg UC vertical members with 200 × 15 mm flange plates.
250 × 100 × 10 mm RHS (rolled hollow section) diagonal members.

6. Primary auditorium trusses
2325 mm deep steel truss spanning between east side perimeter truss and west side columns.
300 × 200 mm × 10 kg RHS top chord.
200 × 200 mm × 10 kg RHS bottom chord.
200 × 100 × 6.3 mm RHS vertical and diagonal members.

7. Access gantry bridges
850 mm or 680 mm wide gantry bridges spanning between primary auditorium trusses.
Two 150 × 100 × 6.3 mm RHS edge members.
Continuous 150 × 90 × 10 mm RSA (rolled steel angle) upstands welded to RHS along both edges.

8. Existing auditorium wall
Existing auditorium concrete blockwork walls demolished down to first floor balcony level.
140 mm inner leaf, 75 mm cavity, 100 mm outer leaf.

9. New auditorium wall
New concrete blockwork wall above first floor balcony level.
140 mm inner leaf, 75 mm cavity, 100 mm outer leaf.

10. Lower ring beam
New minimum 225 mm deep concrete ring beam cast on top of blockwork wall at second balcony level.
Depth varies to take up 70 mm variation in existing blockwork caused by subsidence of raft foundation built on poor ground.

11. Upper ring beam
New 225 mm deep concrete ring beam cast on top of blockwork wall at roof level.

12. New walkways
125 mm thick concrete slab with steel mesh reinforcement on profiled galvanised steel deck.
Walkways act as deep beams to transfer wind loads from façade to east and west ends and into blockwork via ringbeams.
150 × 75 × 12 mm RSA brackets bolted to ring beams and bolted to 150 × 75 × 12 mm RSA brackets welded to steelwork via vertical slotted holes.
Neoprene washers in slotted holes to ensure movement avoid transfer of vertical load to walls.

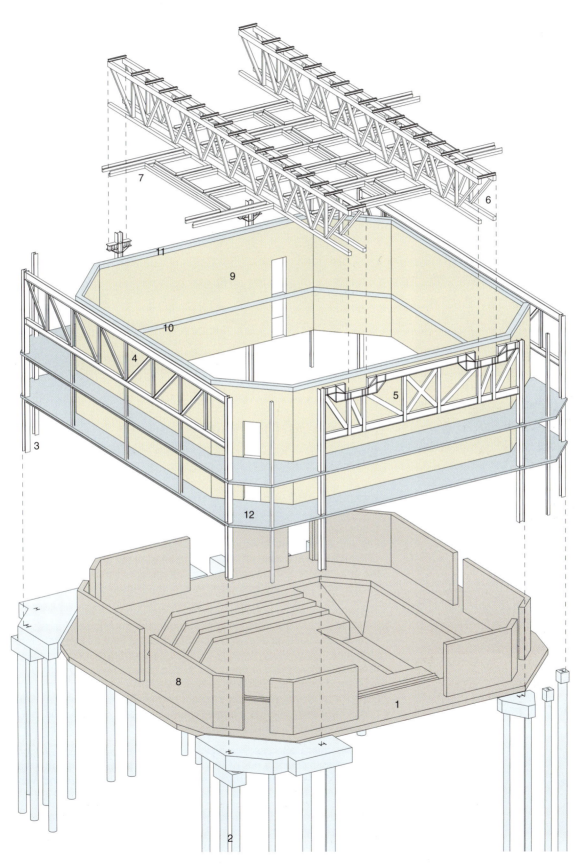

Exploded drawing showing principal auditorium structure

Photo credit: ARC

Photo credit: ARC

Photo credit: ARC

Photo credit: ARC

Photo credit: ARC

House at Dalguise, Fife

Architects: ARC (Architecture, Research, Conservation)

Clay-based materials have been used extensively in a new low-cost house in Fife with a strong sustainability agenda. The house has a simple rectangular plan built off a concrete raft foundation. Most of the accommodation is on the ground floor with a bedroom and storage attic concealed in the steeply pitched roof. The build cost came in at about £650/m^2.

The structural frame is timber – prefabricated in panels with breathable Panelvent sheathing. Often in timber frame construction brick or rendered blockwork is used as a rainscreen with the frame on the inner leaf of the wall, thus losing the opportunity to utilise the thermal mass of the masonry to regulate the internal temperature. In this house the structural timber frame is on the outside, protected by a rainscreen of larch cladding. Instead of lining the studwork walls with a vapour barrier and plasterboard, unfired clay bricks have been used as a non-structural inner leaf providing thermal mass, acoustic insulation, moisture regulation and a robust quality of finish.

The clay bricks, also used for partition walls were made by Errol, a local brick company using a mix of clay and sawdust extruded through a standard brick-making machine. Mortar was made by mixing clay and sand with a small amount of lignosulphate to improve the bond strength.

The walls are finished with a proprietary clay plaster made from clay, sand and plant fibres. The cavity is fully filled with blown cellulose fibre insulation. Moisture can be absorbed into the walls due to the hygroscopic properties of clay, maintaining a more constant level of humidity than conventional construction.

ARC has studied the building in a research project with Dundee and Robert Gordon Universities under the DTI's Partnership In Innovation programme. Among other significant benefits, this has proven the ability of the construction to control internal air relative humidity to between 40 and 60%, and impede condensation of moisture in bathrooms to such an extent as to make extract fans redundant. The clay bricks used offer an 83% embodied energy saving over fired equivalents and produce very little waste.

There are limitations to the use of clay bricks. They are not suitable for structural applications and cannot be used externally as they would absorb too much moisture and swell up. They have to be laid by hand with mortar, a wet trade that takes time, and if they are finished with clay plaster this must be applied by a specially trained applicator. On balance though, unfired clay is an abundant raw material with low embodied energy that can significantly reduce the environmental impact of a building.

Photo credit: ARC

Site plan, scale 1:4000

Ground floor plan, scale 1:300

1. Foundations
150 mm thick reinforced concrete slab thickening to 300 mm at perimeter and below cross walls.
50 mm sand blinding.
150 mm thick consolidated hardcore.

2. Ground floor
19 mm thick solid ash timber floorboards nailed to battens.
60 mm floor void for services filled with weak mix concrete screed.
60 × 40 mm softwood battens at 600 mm centres glued to resilient strips.
10 mm thick resilient felt strips glued to screed.
70 mm fibre-reinforced concrete screed with reinforcing mesh.
15 mm underfloor heating pipes in screed.
120 mm extruded polystyrene insulation.
1200 gauge polythene DPM (damp-proof membrane) laid over slab.

3. Ground floor edge
Concrete blockwork upstand below finished external ground level.
Bituminous damp-proof course lapped with DPM.
Two courses of fired brick in inner and outer leaves.
100 mm polystyrene insulation between inner and outer leaves.

4. Inner leaf
100 mm Errol unfired clay fibre bricks.
Mortar in joints made from clay and sand with a small amount of lignosulphate.
Nominal 18 mm two-coat clay plaster finish.

5. Insulation
200 mm recycled cellulose insulation blown into cavity to completely fill voids in timber frame and cavity.

6. Timber frame
Prefabricated timber frame panels made up from 100 × 50 mm softwood studs at 600 mm centres, 100 × 38 mm softwood wallplates and soleplates, 9 mm Panelvent sheathing screw fixed at 150 mm centres to prevent the timber frame racking.

Stainless steel wall ties between timber frame and clay brick inner leaf.

7. Rainscreen cladding
25 mm thick horizontal untreated larch boards overlapped 25 mm fixed with stainless steel nails to battens.
25 × 50 mm vertical larch battens at 600 mm centres fixed through sheathing to timber frame.
25 mm ventilation gap between battens.
Stainless steel insect mesh fixed between wallplate and larch battens.

8. Windows
Softwood window frames.
Double-glazed sealed unit with 4 mm inner pane, 16 mm cavity and 4 mm low-e outer pane.

9. Window lining
225 × 25 mm larch board lining fixed to softwood battens at head and jambs of windows with stainless steel nails.

10. Roof
Reclaimed Scottish slates laid in diminishing courses.
Felt underlay.
Nominal 20 mm softwood sarking boards with 3 mm gaps.
222 × 47 mm rafters at 600 mm centres in double height area.
Voids between trusses fully filled with blown recycled cellulose insulation.
12.5 mm feather-edged plasterboard with 3 mm clay plaster skim.

11. Roof eaves
Continuous lead eaves flashing dressed over softwood tilting fillet and lapped under breather membrane.
100 mm diameter half-round cast-iron rhone (gutter) painted black.

12. Partition wall
One timber frame cross wall with 100 × 50 mm studs at 450 mm centres.
100 mm Errol unfired clay fibre brick infill between studs.
Nominal 18 mm two-coat clay plaster finish.

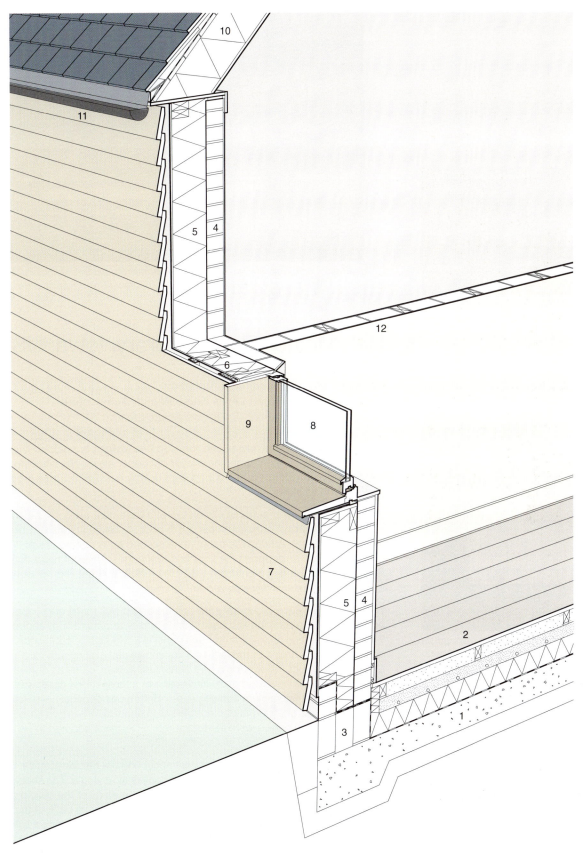

Cut-away section through floor, wall, roof and window

Photo credit: Courtesy David Chipperfield Architects and Des Moines Public Library / Credit Farshid Assassi

Photo credit: Courtesy David Chipperfield Architects and Des Moines Public Library / Credit Farshid Assassi

Photo credit: David Chipperfield Architects

Photo credit: Courtesy David Chipperfield Architects and Des Moines Public Library / Credit Farshid Assassi

Des Moines Public Library, Iowa, USA

Architect: David Chipperfield Architects
Local Architect: Herbert Lewis Kruse Blunck Architecture
Cladding Consultant: W. J. Higgins Associates

The entire façade of the new public library in Des Moines is wrapped in an innovative glass skin incorporating a layer of copper mesh. The cladding provides solar shading, reducing long-term energy costs whilst allowing views out on all sides.

The two-storey concrete frame sits on top of a basement car park. A primary 30 foot (9.1 m) grid of columns is set out to accommodate standard shelving bays of 5 or 6 feet. Around the perimeter a second array of columns at 20 foot centres (6.1 m) supports the floor and roof edges. The roof has a liquid applied asphalt roofing membrane with 25% rubber content laid without a fall and is planted extensively with sedum.

Façade panels with a proprietary aluminium curtain wall frame are suspended on steel brackets from the first floor slab. Brackets at ground floor and roof level provide lateral restraint only. Each panel is 8.5 m high × 1.2 m wide spanning the full height of the façade. Okatech sealed glazing units are bonded with structural silicone to the aluminium frames, either as a vision panel with a clear laminated glass inner pane or as a spandrel panel with insulation and an aluminium backing sheet. Both types of panel have the same outer layer of an expanded copper mesh sheet between two sheets of float glass. The panels were manufactured in Germany and had to be carefully transported halfway around the world.

The copper mesh is expanded from a flat sheet and the resulting lattice of copper is made up of flat strips bent diagonally at an angle. The sheets are fixed with the strips sloping down towards the outside of the building so in effect they act as tiny solar shades. From the inside the back of the copper sheet is in shadow so the sheet is quite transparent despite a light transmission of only 31%. From the outside the copper catches the sun and the glare makes it appear opaque. Overlaying glass enhances the copper's natural sheen and will preserve it from patination.

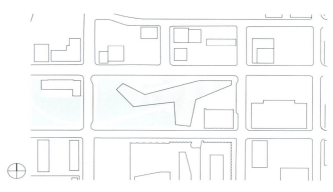

Site plan, scale 1:5000

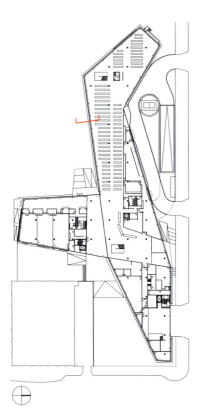

First floor plan, scale 1:1800

1. Concrete frame
355 mm diameter reinforced concrete columns at nominal 6 m centres around perimeter of building.

2. Ground and first floors
460 mm thick reinforced concrete slab.
Spray-on insulation to underside of ground floor slab in car park areas.
400 mm deep floor void forming supply air plenum.
Steel pedestals glued to concrete slab supporting 600 × 600 mm access floor panels.

3. Basement wall
460 mm thick reinforced concrete wall.
Tanking membrane.
50 mm extruded polystyrene insulation.
40 mm thick GFRC (glass fibre reinforced concrete) panel fixed to concrete on galvanised steel stone anchors.
Continuous gravel drainage strip extending 600 mm beyond façade.

4. Roof
355 mm thick reinforced concrete roof slab.
6 mm thick liquid applied rubberised asphalt waterproof membrane.
2 mm rubberised asphalt root barrier.
140 mm thick extruded polystyrene insulation.
5 mm thick water retention mat.
25 mm thick polyethylene 'eggcrate' water retention and drainage layer.
Geotextile fabric filtration membrane.
Soil and extensive sedum green roof.
450 mm wide gravel strip.

5. Roof parapet upstand
380 mm high × 225 mm thick reinforced concrete upstand.
Liquid applied rubberised asphalt waterproof membrane.
75 mm vertical rigid insulation.
12 mm exterior grade plywood.
Waterproof flashing dressed down over plywood and lapped over roof membrane.

6. Roof parapet coping
3 mm Kynar coated folded aluminium coping with fixing angle welded to inside hooked over clips bolted to curtain wall frame.
30 mm rigid insulation.
18 mm external grade plywood on softwood packers.

7. First floor curtain wall support brackets
300 × 160 × 76 mm deep pockets in 1st floor concrete slab at 1220 mm centres.
250 × 165 × 50 mm high steel curtain wall support angles fixed into slab pockets with two cast-in bolts and slotted holes for adjustment.

Two steel hangers bolted either side of each mullion, hooked over support angle and bolted in place.

8. Roof level curtain wall supports
152 × 89 × 10 mm unequal steel angle brackets fixed to channel cast into concrete upstand to provide lateral restraint only.
Top box section of curtain wall frame bolted to angle via slotted holes to allow vertical movement.

9. Ground level curtain wall supports
650 × 105 mm cantilevered anchor supports bolted to channels cast into slab at 1220 mm centres.
250 × 165 × 50 mm high steel curtain wall support angle brackets bolted to anchor supports to provide lateral restraint only.
Two steel hangers bolted either side of each mullion, hooked over support angle and bolted in place.

10. Plinth
1210 × 570 × 40 mm thick vertical GFRC panel fixed to vertical curtain wall mullion with galvanised steel cleats.
1210 × 405 mm horizontal closer panel made from folded perforated galvanised steel sheet.
75 mm thick galvanised pressed steel insulated panels horizontally and vertically.

11. Curtain wall frames
124 × 76 mm extruded aluminium box-section frames at ground floor, first floor and roof levels.
Vertical extruded aluminium channels on each panel interlock to form one vertical 124 × 76 mm mullion.

12. Glazed vision panel sealed unit
8 mm low-iron outer pane with copper coloured frit around edges to conceal structural silicone.
2 mm cavity with expanded copper mesh secured in corners with spots of silicone.
8 mm solar control glass with low-e coating.
16 mm air cavity.
10 mm laminated inner pane comprising two panes 5 mm float glass and 0.76 mm PVB (polyvinylbutyral) interlayer.

13. Glazed spandrel panel
8 mm low-iron outer pane with copper coloured frit around edges to conceal structural silicone.
2 mm cavity with expanded copper mesh secured in corners with spots of silicone.
8 mm solar control glass with low-e coating.
30 mm air cavity.
120 mm rigid insulation.
3 mm folded aluminium backing sheet.

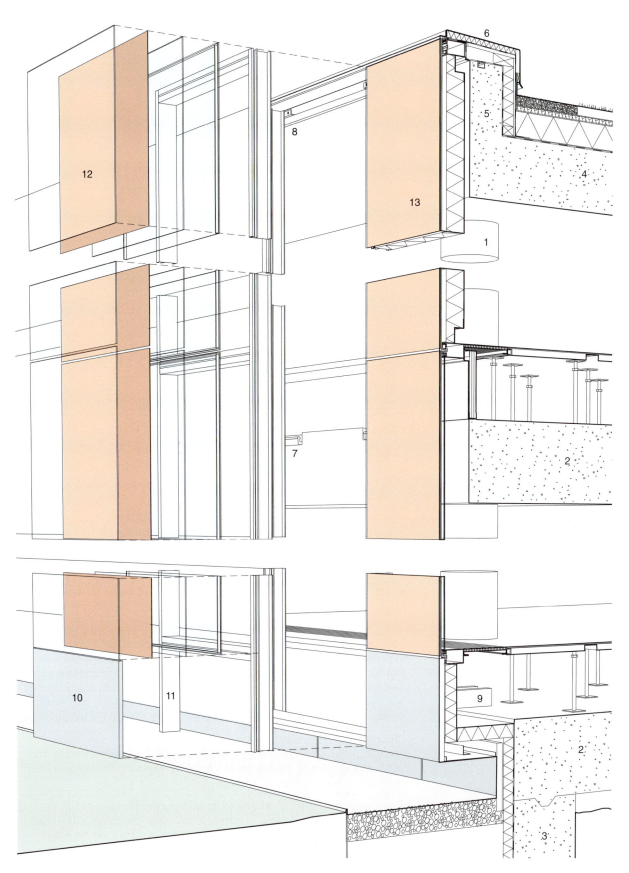

Exploded section through typical façade

London Centre for Nanotechnology, University College London

Architects: Feilden Clegg Bradley Architects
Structural, Mechanical and Electrical Engineer: Buro Happold

The Nanotechnology building has eight floors of laboratories and offices dedicated to interdisciplinary research in atomic scale devices and materials. It provides a centre where electrical engineers, physicists, chemists, biologists and medics can work together on projects in highly serviced, clean-room standard research labs. The two main elevations to Gordon Street and the UCL courtyard have elaborate, double skinned, metal façades designed to be representative of the research work carried out within.

An in-situ concrete sway frame with exposed painted slabs provides passive temperature regulation through its thermal mass. A sway frame gains its stability from rigid column-to-slab moment connections avoiding the need for downstand beams. Upstand shear walls along the perimeter help protect the building from external vibration and the main stair and lift are isolated from the surrounding structure to reduce transfer of vibration to the laboratories.

Cooling is achieved with chilled beams and the building is fully mechanically ventilated with a thermal wheel heat recovery system. Heating comes from UCL's district heating system and the building meets the Breeam excellent standard for commercial office buildings.

The façade to Gordon Street has a tripartite composition picking up the divisions of the neighbouring buildings in the conservation area. The base is clad in Portland stone and the two upper stories are glazed full height with vertical solar shading fins. The central section of the façades is layered, consisting of an inner stainless steel rainscreen clad wall with fixed windows, steel maintenance walkways and an outer layer of perforated brises soleil.

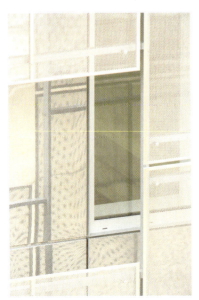

Photo credit: Tim Soar / Tim Soar Photography

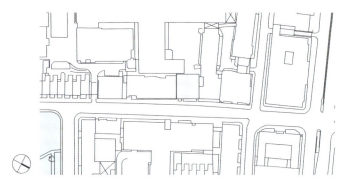

Site plan, scale 1:3000

The walkways span between the inner concrete structure and a line of outrigger steel T-columns in line with the brises soleil.

A pattern of dots the same as the perforations in the brises soleil has been bead blasted at an angle on to the mirror polished stainless steel of the inner rainscreen. One pattern is visible through the other, creating a Moiré pattern, an effect used to demonstrate wave interference. A slight change in the position of the observer creates a large-scale change in the pattern. Lighting concealed in the walkways enhances the effect so the façade is constantly changing from night to day and in different weather conditions.

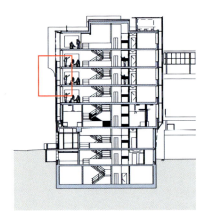

East – west section with area of detail shown in red, scale 1:750

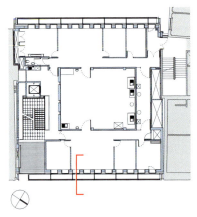

Third floor plan with area of detail shown in red, scale 1:500

1. Structure
300 mm thick reinforced concrete floor slab.
300 mm thick × 500 mm wide reinforced concrete columns at 1.5 m centres.
300 mm thick × 800 mm high reinforced concrete shear walls between columns.

2. Rainscreen cladding
Liquid applied bituminous vapour barrier painted on to concrete.
1.5 mm thick mirror finish stainless steel panels with bead blasted dot pattern fixed back to concrete with 6 mm thick thermally broken adjustable aluminium support brackets.
150 mm mineral fibre insulation with dense weather resisting outer layer cut around brackets.
50 mm air gap.

3. Fixed glazing
Prefabricated window subframe made from 190 × 150 × 2 mm thick galvanised steel angle bolted to concrete with expanding anchors.
Vapour barrier bonded to subframe.
68 × 48 mm thermally broken aluminium window frames screwed to subframe.
24 mm thick double glazed sealed units.

4. Internal linings
Insulated plasterboard dry lining on metal studs.
Vapour barrier.
50 mm thick painted softwood cill board.
50 mm insulation below cill.

5. Vertical channel
100 × 50 × 3 mm aluminium feature channel fixed to concrete on aluminium brackets.

6. Walkway support brackets
Galvanised steel adjustable bracket assembly comprising 152 × 89 × 250 mm long channel bolted to paired 150 × 90 × 15 mm angles bolted to concrete with expanding anchors.
150 × 90 stainless steel T brackets bolted to channel via structural thermal break block.

7. Walkway
Painted galvanised steel walkway in 2950 × 605 mm sections bolted to support brackets.
Each section made from 100 × 16 mm flat ends welded to 100 × 65 × 10 mm front and rear angles supporting 30 mm thick stainless steel grating on rubber isolating strip.

8. Vertical walkway support columns
127 × 152 mm mild steel T section columns fixed to walkway with M16 bolts.

9. Vertical channel
100 × 50 × 2 mm stainless steel feature channel fixed to columns with M5 button head fixings and nylon isolating washers.

10. Brise Soleil support frame
50 × 20 mm mild steel intermediate supports.
Horizontal rail angles welded up from 40 × 15 mm and 40 × 10 mm mild steel flats and bolted to vertical supports and columns.
High-performance paint finish.

11. Brise Soleil
1.5 mm brushed stainless steel panels with circular perforations and 20 mm folded edges.
Panels fixed with stainless steel button head fixings via 15 mm diameter tube spacers.

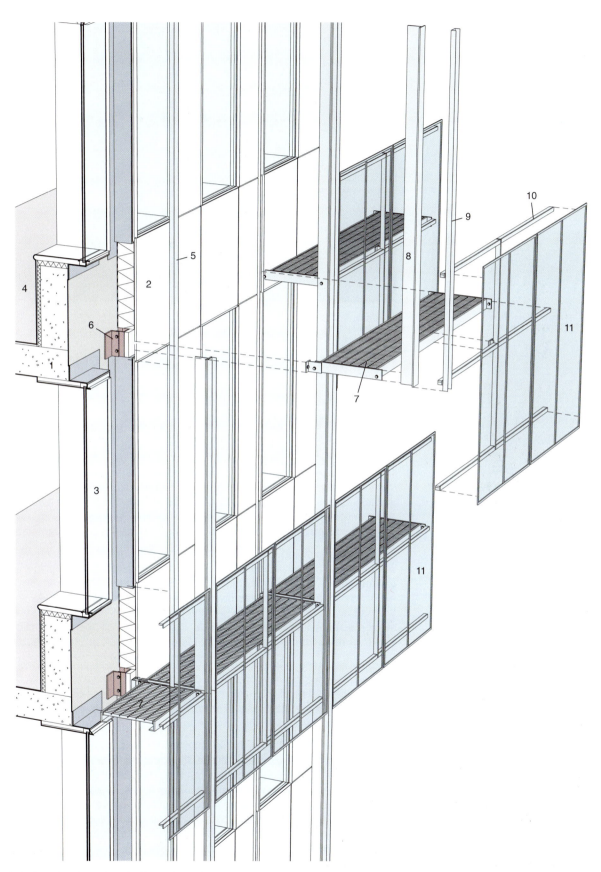

Exploded section through typical bay of east façade

Newington Green House, London

Architect: Prewett Bizley Architects
Structural Engineer: Price & Myers

The 99 square metre house occupies a tiny derelict site at the end of a Victorian terrace in north London. Monolithic walls with no visible lintels or architraves give the house a strong defensive character against the harsh urban environment. The second floor bay window projects out 200 mm beyond the brickwork on a steel structure which also supports the brick parapet above.

Internally the exposed brick walls and roof joists are painted white providing a rich textural background to more crafted timber elements such as the window linings made from 18 mm birch plywood. Masonry walls and an exposed concrete ground slab give the house a high thermal mass. Air warmed by the underfloor heating in the ground floor is drawn up the stair by stack effect providing constant passive ventilation. Small opening vents can divert warm air from under the rooflight into the bedroom or up the stairs.

The staircase rises three stories through the rough brick shell and is lined with book shelves and hidden cupboards. 36 mm thick birch plywood treads span from a central spine of 95 × 38 mm Douglas fir studs to rest on 40 × 25 mm steel angles bolted to the walls. The angles slot into a groove in the end of the tread which was filled with silicone to hold it in place and eliminate the possibility of squeaking.

All the components were made off site and the treads were made over-long so they could be cut precisely to size on site. The central studwork was made in seven triangular sections with a 7 mm tolerance zone between each section. Two cedar shingles were inserted from either side to pack between the sections, their wedge shape allowing very precise adjustment. The treads tie each section of studwork to a wall and are located on the studwork with dowels. The inner leaf of brick is not plumb and the plan changes subtly between each half-level so a very accurate site survey had to be carried out including measuring 3-dimensional diagonals.

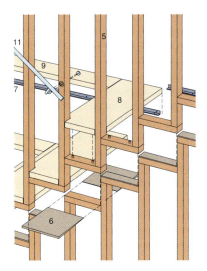

Detail of stair construction

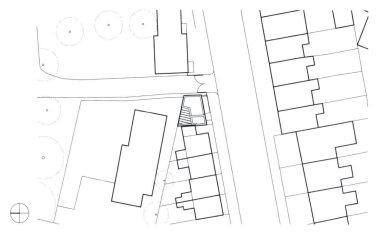

Site plan, scale 1:1000

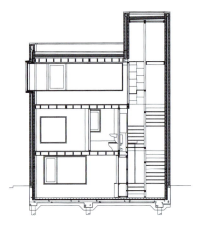

North – south section, scale 1:200

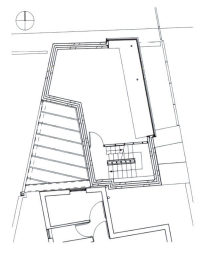

Second floor plan, scale 1:200

1. Ground floor
50 mm floating concrete screed with polypropylene fibre and mesh reinforcement. Underfloor heating pipes.
Polythene vapour barrier.
50 mm extruded polystyrene insulation.
150 mm reinforced concrete slab spanning between ground beams on mini-piles.

2. External walls below ground level
102 mm load-bearing brickwork inner leaf.
50 mm expanded polystyrene insulation.
150 mm thick reinforced concrete upstand.
Waterproof membrane externally.

3. External walls above ground level
102 mm load-bearing brickwork inner leaf.
50 mm PIS (polyisocyanurate) insulation
50 mm air gap.
102 mm face brick outer leaf.

4. Landings
38 mm birch faced plywood landing pre-fabricated oversized and cut to fit on site.
Plywood screwed to joists from underside using metal angle brackets to conceal fixings.
Paired 175 × 50 mm softwood trimmer joists at landing edge.
175 × 50 mm softwood joists bolted to brickwork on other sides.
12.5 mm fire-resisting plasterboard screwed to underside of joists with plaster skim coat.

5. Studwork spine
95 × 38 mm douglas fir studs at 250 mm centres vertically glued and screwed into seven triangular sections off-site.
Studwork sections were made 7 mm short to allow for packing between each section.

6. Packers
Tapering cedar roof shingles pushed between studwork sections from both sides and glued to pack each section up to required height.
Studwork sections screwed down through packers into studwork section below.

7. Wall angle brackets
40 × 25 × 4 mm mild steel angles bolted to brick wall or screwed into timber studwork to support stair treads and shelves.
Brackets drilled with over-sized holes to allow adjustment to level treads.

8. Stair treads
286 mm wide × 36 mm thick birch faced plywood treads pre-cut oversized and cut to length exactly on site.
6 mm groove in one end to slot onto angle.
Groove filled with silicone to fix tread in place.
Each tread located on two timber dowels glued into central studwork spine.

9. Shelves
225 mm wide × 36 mm thick birch faced plywood shelves with groove in rear filled with silicone and slotted over concealed angles.
10 mm diameter stainless steel threaded bar hanger bolted into landing joists to support longer shelves with nut and washer recessed into underside of shelf.

10. Alternate tread stair
2485 × 1530 × 800 mm wide prefabricated staircase made up from biscuited and glued 36 mm birch faced plywood pieces.
Lowest riser of stair extends down to form 2nd floor landing edge and bears on 100 × 100 × 8 mm mild steel angle bolted to landing trimmer joists via timber batten secret-fixed into rear of riser.
Top riser extends up to form 3rd floor landing edge and bears on landing trimmer joists via 25 × 40 mm mild steel angle secret-fixed into rear of riser.

11. Handrails
Clear lacquered 25 mm diameter steel circular hollow section handrail.
12 mm diameter brackets welded to handrail and inserted in holes in timber studs.
Brackets have 30 mm diameter washer welded around shaft to locate them in studwork and are clamped from behind with pan-head bolts recessed into opposite face of studwork.

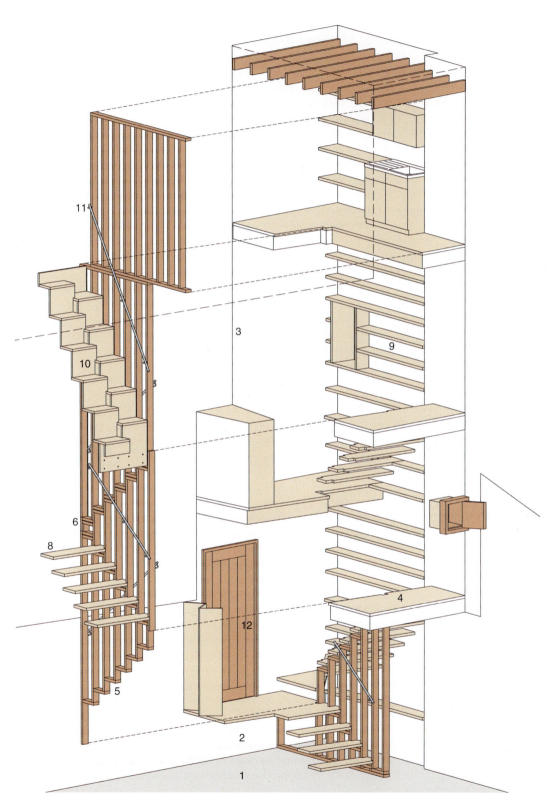

Exploded drawing of staircase

Project credits

The introduction and accompanying text for each project were written by Graham Bizley. The detail illustration for each project was drawn by Graham Bizley except for the drawing for The Public which was drawn by Alsop Architects and Graham Bizley. All other drawings were supplied by the architects or engineers. I would like to thank the architects and clients for allowing their projects to be published in this book and for supplying the necessary information. The photographer for each image used is credited with the image and I am most grateful to them for allowing their images to be used.

Why One Thing, not Another?

Graham Bizley
Graham Bizley
RES/Fusion
Graham Bizley
Graham Bizley
Grimshaw
Keith Williams Architects
Tim Soar Photography
Graham Bizley

Individual Project Credits

Verulamium Hypocaust Building, St Albans

Client: St Albans City and District Council
Architect: muf architecture/art
Structural Engineer: Atelier One
M&E Services Engineer: Atelier 10
Quantity Surveyor: McBains Cooper
Cladding Consultant: Smart Crosby
Shell Supplier: Specialist Aggregates

Photographs: Jason Lowe, Muf Architecture/Art

Bedford School Library, Bedford

Client: Bedford School
Architect: Eric Parry Architects
Structural Engineer: Adams Kara Taylor
Services Engineer: Michael Popper Associates
Quantity Surveyor: Davis Langdon & Everest
Main Contractor: T&E Neville

Photographs:
Peter Cook – http://www.petercookphoto.com
Eric Parry Architects

Digital Studio at Oxford Brookes School of Architecture, Oxford

Client: Oxford Brookes University
Architect: Niall McLaughlin Architects
Quantity Surveyor: Sworn King & Partners
Contractor: EW Beard Ltd
Structural Engineer: Packman Lucas
M&E: Richard Cleaver Ridge

Photographs:
Nicholas Kane – http://www.nickkane.co.uk

Trevision Production Building, Vienna, Austria

Client: Trevision GmbH
Architect: Querkraft Architekten
Structural Engineer: Vasko & Partner, Vienna
Services Engineer: PME, Ollern
Lighting design: Konzept Licht Steindl, Vienna
Site Co-ordinator: Wolfgang Kutzelnig
Main Contractor: Bader-bau, Horitschon

Photographs:
Hertha Hurnaus – http://www.hertha-hurnaus.com/
Querkraft Architekten

Crop Store, Renewable Energy Centre, Kings Langley, Hertfordshire

Client: Renewable Energy Systems Ltd
Architect: Studio E Architects
M&E Services Engineer: Max Fordham LLP
Structural Engineer: Dewhurst Macfarlane and Partners
Quantity Surveyor: A&S Friend
Project Manager: King Sturge
Main Contractor: Willmott Dixon Construction
EU Partners: Esbensen Consulting Engineers; Netherlands Energy Research
Foundation (ECN); Shell Solar energy BV

Photographs:
RES/Fusion
Studio E Architects Ltd

Fountain on the Nikolaikirchhof, Leipzig, Germany

Client: City of Leipzig
Architect: David Chipperfield Architects
Structural Engineer: Ingenieurgruppe Bauen
Services Engineer: Jaeger, Mornhinweg + Partner Ingenieurgesellschaft

Photographs:
Jörg von Bruchhausen – http://www.bruchhausen-fotografie.de
David Chipperfield Architects

Youl Hwa Dang Publishing House, Paju Book City, Seoul, South Korea

Client: Mr Yi, Ki-Ung – President, Youl Hwa Dang Publishing Co.
Architects: Architecture Research Unit, London with Florian Beigel
Architects
(Florian Beigel, Philip Christou, Base Sang Soo, Min Jun Kee) and
Metropolitan Architecture Research
Unit, Seoul (Kim Jong Kyu, Kang Kyoung Hwa. Choi Jong Hun)
Structural Engineer: Seoul Structural Engineering
Services Engineer: Han Yang TEC & Ko Do Engineering
Main Contractor: Dong Nyuk construction

Photographs:
Jonathan Lovekin – +44 (0)1796 483308
Kang Kyoung Hwa, MARU
Philip Christou, ARU

The Public Gallery, West Bromwich

Client: The Public
Architect: Alsop Architects
Structural Engineer: Adams Kara Taylor
M&E services engineer: Battle McCarthy
Acoustic Engineer: Sandy Brown Associates
Main Contractor: Galliford Try
Cladding Contractor: Richardson Roofing Ltd

Photographs:
Roderick Coyne
Alsop Architects

Kingsdale School Auditorium, Dulwich, London

Client: London Borough of Southwark, Education
Architect: dRMM Architects
Structural Engineer: Michael Hadi Associates
Building Services Engineer: Fulcrum Consulting
Quantity Surveyor: Appleyard + Trew
Project Manager: Southwark Building Design Services
Acoustic Consultant: Flemming and Barron
Collaborator for light, air and sound 'cannon': Atelier von Lieshout
Main Contractor: Galliford Try Construction
Specialist Contractor and Supplier for timber auditorium pod shell: Gordon
Cowley, Timber Engineering Connections

Photographs:
Alex de Rijke
Michael Mack
de Rijke Marsh Morgan

Moggerhanger House, Bedfordshire

Client: Moggerhanger House Preservation Trust supported by the Heritage
Lottery Fund
Architect: Inskip & Jenkins Architects

Structural Engineer: Ralph Mills
Main Contractor: E Bowman & Sons
Paint Analyst: Catherine Hassal
Paint Supplier: Craig & Rose
Ironwork: Ridgeway Forge
Hydraulic lime supplier: Telling Limes

Photographs:
Richard Holttum – +44 (0)20 7251 5116
Peter Inskip, Stephen Gee

Tower of London Environs, London

Client: Historic Royal Palaces
Architect: Stanton Williams
Structural and M&E Services Engineer: Ove Arup & Partners
Quantity Surveyor: Gardiner & Theobold
Soft Landscaping Consultant: Churchman Landscape
Lighting Consultant: LAPD
Traffic Consultant: Pell Frischmann
Disability Consultant: All Clear Design
Archaeological Consultant: Keevil Heritage Consultancy
Archaeological Investigations: Oxford Archaeological Unit
Visitor Flow Consultants: Crowdsafe Ltd
Graphics/signage: Aukett Brockliss Guy
Main Contractor: Wallis
Stonework Subcontractor: Szerelmey
Groundwork Subcontractor: Gabriel Civil Engineering
M&E Subcontractor: RTT Engineering

Photographs: Morley von Sternberg – http://www.vonsternberg.com/

City and County Museum, Lincoln

Architect: Panter Hudspith Architects
Structural Engineer: Price & Myers
M&E Services Engineer: Arup
Quantity Surveyor: Burke Hunter Adams
Project Manager: Focus Consultants
Exhibition Designer: Event Communications
Clerk of Works: Hickton Consultants
Gallery Consultant: Art Handling
Main Contractor: Caddick Construction Ltd
Concrete Subcontractor: Northfield Construction
Stone Contractor: J.W. Smith

Photographs:
Hélène Binet – http://www.helenebinet.com/
Panter Hudspith Architects

A13 Artscape Project – Pump Control House, Barking and Dagenham

Client: London Borough of Baking and Dagenham
Architect: Tom dePaor
Lighting Design: Clare Brew
Technical advice: Quo Vadis

Photographs:
Hufton + Crow – http://www.huftonandcrow.com/

Metropolitan Cathedral Campus, Liverpool

Client: Neptune Developments with the Liverpool Roman Catholic Archdiocese
Architect: Falconer Chester Hall Architects
Landscape Architect: Landscape Projects
Structural Engineers: Bingham Davis
M&E Engineers: The Davis Partnership
Quantity Surveyor: Tweeds
Principal Contractor: HBG Construction

Photographs:
shaw + shaw – http://www.shawandshaw.co.uk/
Falconer Chester Hall Architects

St Paul's Old Ford Church, Bow, London

Client: St Paul with St Mark PCC
Architect: Matthew Lloyd Architects LLP
Quantity Surveyor: Gardiner & Theobald
Structural Engineer: Price & Myers
M&E Engineer: Arup
Building Control Consultant: Butler & Young
Contractor: Balfour Beatty Refurbishment Ltd

Photographs:
ReUrba
Matthew Lloyd Architects

Friars Halt Studio, Battle, East Sussex

Client: Private
Architect: Inglis Badrashi Loddo Architects
Structural Engineer: Price and Myers
Contractor: George Stone Ltd
Glazed Screen: Icklesham Joinery Ltd
Bricks: Sussex Brick

Photographs:
David Grandorge – d.grandorge@londonmet.ac.uk

Novy Dvur Monastery, Czech Republic

Client: Monastery of Saint Lieu Sept-Fons
Architect: John Pawson Architects
Executive Architect: Atelier Soukup, Pilsen
Collaborating Architect: Denton Corker Marshall, London
Landscape Architect: BBUK Landscape Architecture, London
Structural Engineers: Jindrich Rines, Prague, RAVAL v.o.s., Pilsen
Lighting Design: Isometrix Lighting & Design, London, ETNA spol. s.r.o., Prague
Contractor: Starkon CZ a.s., Jihlava

Photographs:
Štěpán Bartoš – http://www.fotobartos.cz/

Summerhouse, Stoke Newington, London

Client: Private
Architect: Ullmayer Sylvester Architects
Structural Engineer: BTA Structural Design

Photographs:
Kilian O'Sullivan/VIEW – http://www.light-room.co.uk/

Imperial War Museum Visitors Centre, Duxford, Cambridgeshire

Client: Imperial War Museum Duxford
Architect: London bloc
Building Shell Architect: HOK
Project Manager: Davis Langdon Everest
Quantity Surveyor: Davis Langdon Everest
Structural Engineer: Connell Mott MacDonald
Main Contractor: Mivan
Lighting Consultant: Lighting and Product Design (LAPD)

Photographs:
Edmund Sumner/VIEW
London bloc

Unicorn Theatre, London

Client: Unicorn Theatre for Children
Architect: Keith Williams Architects
Structural Engineer: Arup
M&E Services Engineer: Arup
Quantity Surveyor: Bucknall Austin
Theatre consultant: Theatre Projects Consultants
Acoustician: Arup Acoustics
Access Consultant: Buro Happold
Main Contractor: Mansell

Photographs:
Hélène Binet – http://www.helenebinet.com/
Keith Williams Architects

Museum of World Culture, Gothenburg, Sweden

Client: Statens Fastighetsverk (National Property Board of Sweden)
Architect: Brisac Gonzalez Architects
Glass Consultant: Akiboye Conolly Architects
Structural Engineer: Flygfältsbyrån AB, Anthony Hunt Associates
Mechanical Services Engineer: Bengt Dahlgren
Electrical Engineer: J&W Sjölanders
Lighting Design: Speirs and Major Associates

Photographs:
Hélène Binet – http://www.helenebinet.com/

Alpine House, Kew Gardens, London

Client: The Royal Botanic Gardens, Kew
Architect: Wilkinson Eyre Architects Ltd
Greenhouse Engineer: Green-Mark International
Quantity Surveyor: Fanshawe
Structural Engineer: Dawhurst MacFarlane & Partners
M&E Services Engineers: Atelier Ten
Planning Supervisor: Goyne Adams
Steel/glass contractor: Tuchschmid Constructa AG
Ground-works Contractor: Killby & Gayford
Shading Contractor: Osen Structures Ltd

Photographs:
Hélène Binet – http://www.helenebinet.com/

Westfield Student Village, Queen Mary, University of London

Client: Queen Mary, University of London
Architect: Feilden Clegg Bradley Architects
Structural Engineer: Adams Kara Taylor
Services Engineer: Max Fordham & Partners
Quantity Surveyor: Turner & Townsend
Acoustic Designer: Paul Gillieron Acoustic Design
Main Contractor: Laing O'Rourke Construction

Photographs:
Peter Cook – http://www.petercookphoto.com/
Will Pryce – http://willpryce.com
Feilden Clegg Bradley Architects

Carlisle Lane Housing, Waterloo, London

Client: Pringle + Richards LLP
Architect: Pringle Richards Sharratt Architects
Structural Engineer: Alan Baxter & Associates
Timber Frame and Timber Cladding: Eurban Limited with Finnforest Merk
(engineering, manufacture and erection)
General Contractor: D F Keane Limited

Photographs:
Edmund Sumner/VIEW – http://www.edmundsumner.co.uk/
Eurban

National Gallery East Wing, London

Client: The National Gallery
Architect: Dixon Jones Architects
Project Manager: Davis Langdon & Everest
Quantity Surveyors: Gardiner & Theobald
Structural Engineer: Alan Baxter & Associates
M&E Services Engineer: Andrew Reid & Partners
Historic Renovation: Purcell Miller Tritton
Acoustics/AV: Sound Research Laboratories
Lighting Consultant: BDP Lighting
Planning Supervisor: PFB Construction Management

Retail Designer: Din Associates
Fire Consultant: Kingfell Fire Protection
Access Consultant: AD&M Ltd
Signage Consultant: Holmes Wood Consultancy
Lift Consultant: GW Lift & Escalator Consulting Engineers
Archaeology: The Museum of London
Main Contractor: Wates Construction Ltd

Photographs:
Morley von Sternberg – http://www.vonsternberg.com/

National Assembly for Wales, Cardiff

Client: National Assembly for Wales
Architect: Richard Rogers Partnership
Design & Build Contractor: Taylor Woodrow Construction
Structural Engineer: Arup
Environmental Engineer: BDSP
Civil Engineer: Arup
Landscape Architect: Gillespies LLP
Access Consultant: Vin Goodwin Access Consultant

Photographs:
Redshift Photography – http://www.redshift-photography.co.uk/

Queens Road Community Centre, Walthamstow, London

Client: London Borough of Waltham Forest with English Partnerships & Sure Start
Architect: Greenhill Jenner Architects
Project Manager: Dearle & Henderson
Structural Engineer: Fluid Structures
Services Engineers: Max Fordham & Partners
Quantity Surveyor: KMCS
Landscape Architect for nursery play area: Planet Earth

Photographs:
Charlotte Wood – http://www.charlottewood.com
Greenhill Jenner Architects

Sky Ear

Designer: Usman Haque, Haque Design + Research
Assistants: Shade Abdul, Ai Hasegawa
Host: National Maritime Museum, Greenwich
Structural advice: David Crookes, Fluid Structures Engineers and Technical Designers
Financial assistance: the Daniel Langlois Foundation for Art, Science and Technology
Electronics & B2B network by Seth Garlock, Senseinate Inc
Software by Rolf Pixley, Anomalous Research Ltd
Microcontrollers provided by Texas Instruments Inc
Carbon fibre tubing for framework by RBJ Plastics
Mobile phone provider: Alcatel

Photographs:
David Rothschild – davidroths@aol.com
Ai Hasegawa
National Maritime Museum

Salvation Army Chapel, London

Client: The Salvation Army
Chapel Architect: Carpenter Lowings Architects
Developer: Hines UK
Building Architect: Sheppard Robson
Building Engineer: Ove Arup & Partners
Contractor: Bowmer & Kirkland
Façade Contractor: Dane Architectural Systems

Photographs:
Tim Soar – http://www.valencyengine.co.uk/
Luke Lowings

BBC Broadcasting House, London

Client: BBC
Architect: MJP Architects
Structural Engineer: Whitbybird
Façade Engineer: Whitbybird
M&E Services Engineer: Faber Maunsel
Acoustic Design: Bickerdike Allen
Contractor: Bovis Lend Lease
Steel & glass façades: MERO UK
Aluminium windows: GIG Fassadenbau
Precast stone-faced panels: Techrete UK
Hand-set stone: PAYE Stone

Photographs:
Tim Crocker – http://www.timcrocker.co.uk/
Whitby Bird
MacCormac Jamieson Pritchard Architects

Education Resource Centre, Eden Project, Cornwall

Client: Eden Project Ltd.
Architect: Nicholas Grimshaw & Partners
Structural Engineer: SKM Anthony Hunts
M&E Services Engineer: Buro Happold
Quantity Surveyor: David Langdon
Landscape Architect: Land Use Consultants
Main Contractor: McAlpine Joint Venture
Project Supervisor: Scott Wilson

Photographs:
Adam Parker – http://www.buildingimages.eu
Nicholas Grimshaw & Partners

Hunterian Museum at the Royal College of Surgeons, London

Client: Trustees of the Hunterian Museum and the Royal College of Surgeons
Architect: Julian Bicknell & Associates
Exhibition Design: John Ronayne
Structural Engineer: Faber Maunsell
M&E Services Engineer: Faber Manusell

Lighting Consultant: Lighting Services Partnership
Main Contractor: Beck Interiors
Case design and manufacture: Netherfield Visual ltd
Fibre optics: Museum & Gallery Lighting

Photographs:
Morley von Sternberg – http://www.vonsternberg.com/

Galleria Fashion Mall, Seoul, South Korea

Client: Hanwha Corporation
Architect: UN studio – Ben van Berkel and Caroline Bos
Lighting Design: Arup Lighting – Rogier van der Heide
Executive Architect: Rah Architecture, Korea
Detailed Lighting Design: Arup Lighting
Lighting Hardware: Xilver BV
Control Systems: E:Cue

Photographs:
Christian Richters – chrichters @aol.com
Rogier van der Heide / Arup

Wembley Stadium Arch, London

Client: Wembley National Stadium Ltd
Architect: World Stadium Team (Foster & Partners with HOK Sport and
Venue & Events)
Structural Engineer: Mott Stadium Consortium
M&E Services Engineer: Mott Stadium Consortium
Main Contractor: Multiplex
Arch Steel Supplier: Corus
Arch Steelwork Contractor: Cleveland Bridge

Photographs:
Nigel Young / Foster + Partners

Victoria & Albert Museum Courtyard, London

Client: Victoria & Albert Museum
Director of projects, V&A Musuem: Gwyn Miles
Landscape Architect: Kim Wilkie Associates
Project Construction Manager: Bovis Lend Lease
Structural Engineer: Dewhurst MacFarlane
M&E Services Engineer: Arup
Stonemason: S McConnell & Sons
Stone flxing: Szerelmey
York stone supplier: Johnsons of Wellfield
Chinese red sandstone supplier: Farrars
Lighting Design: AC Lighting and Patrick Woodroffe
Planting & maintenances: ISS Waterers

Photographs:
Kim Wilkie

Young Vic Theatre, London

Architect: Haworth Tompkins Architects
Structural Engineer: Jane Wernick Associates
Project Manager: Buro 4
Mechanical Engineering: Max Fordham
Acoustic Engineer: Paul Gillieron Acoustic Design
Theatre Consultants: Studio Tod-Lecat and Theatre Project Consultants
QS: David Langdon

Photographs:
Philip Vile – http://www.philipvile.com/
Haworth Tompkins

House at Dalguise, Fife

Client: Private
Architect: ARC Chartered Architects
Unfired Brick Supplier: Errol Brick

Photographs:
ARC

Des Moines Public Library, Iowa, USA

Client: Des Moines Public Library
Architect: David Chipperfield Architects
Local Architect: Herbert Lewis Kruse Blunck Architecture
Façade Consultant: W. J. Higgins & Associates, Inc.: Wes Higgins
Structural Engineer: Jane Wernick Associates
Local Structural Engineer: Shuck-Britson
Services Engineer: Arup
Local Services Engineer: KJWW
General Contractor: The Weitz Company
Glass Façade Supplier: Okalux, Germany

Photographs:
Courtesy David Chipperfield Architects and Des Moines Public Library /
Credit Farshid Assassi – http://www.assassi.com/

London Centre for Nanotechnology, University College London

Client: University College London
Architect: Feilden Clegg Bradley Architects
Structural Engineer: Buro Happold
M&E Services Engineer: Buro Happold
Quantity Surveyor: Edmond Shipway & Partners
Planning Supervisor: Buro Happold

Photographs:
Tim Soar – http://www.valencyengine.co.uk/

Newington Green House, London

Client: Graham Bizley
Architect: Prewett Bizely Architects
Structural Engineer: Price & Myers
Main Contractor: GAP (Special Works) ltd.
Staircase timber components: Creative Craftsmen
Stair handrail: Ray Smith – RS Projects
Staircase construction: Graham Bizley, Robert Prewett, Sam Tyler
Windows: Sparkford Sawmills

Photographs:
Kilian O'Sullivan – http://www.light-room.co.uk/